CONTENTS

Author's Note vii

1. The Suru and Its People 1
2. Journey into the Valley 8
3. Shaktiman with Wings 16
4. A Way to Kargil 24
5. The Small Field Hospital 31
6. The First Night 43
7. A Proper Reception 48
8. Mind over Matter 56
9. Major Cases 63
10. A Feast of Bullets 72
11. Tasting Menu 82
12. A Shocking Discovery 93
13. Meeting the Press 99
14. A Morale Boost 107
15. Visitors 116
16. Celebrities 122
17. Shelters and Rations 126
18. The Brave Indian Soldier 132
19. Enemy Soldiers 138
20. The Special Casualty 142
21. Pakistan's Treachery 150
22. Hard Choices 156

Contents

23. The Major Returns   163
24. Flight to Srinagar   167
25. The Suru's Eternal Flow   177

Acknowledgements   183
About the Author   185

Advance Praise for *The Kargil War Surgeon's Testimony*

'As the first military surgeon on call at Kargil in the summer of 1999 – when Pakistani troops, disguised as goatherds, crossed over the Line of Control and besieged critical Indian peaks – Arup Ratan Basu toiled to rescue nearly 250 of our valiant soldiers from the jaws of death. One can only imagine how helpless he, trained to be a lifesaver, must have felt seeing a steadfast stream of young men marching to their deaths at those inhospitable heights – that too in a war not of their nation's making.

In Basu's view, it's not so much about the futility of war as its untold human cost, which gets muffled beneath the nationalist pomp and clamour of any war effort – even one like Kargil, undertaken in self-defence. Yet for the parents who lose their sons, wives their husbands and children their fathers, this is the *only* real consequence of war. And perhaps on no one's conscience do these deaths weigh more heavily than on a doctor's – who, for no fault of his own, could not prevent them.

A military doctor with a poet's sensitivity and talent for lyrical expression, Arup Ratan Basu has composed a haunting elegy to the lives lost and blood spilt at Kargil. And as a powerful, poignant and heart-wrenching indictment of the debilitating cost of war, *The Kargil War Surgeon's Testimony* ought to be read – and remembered.'

Shashi Tharoor, Member of Parliament

'Basu captures the human face of the Kargil war, treating the war-wounded including a Pakistani soldier. Touching, easy to read, an interesting perspective.'

Lt General (Retd) Vinod Bhatia,
former Director General of Military Operations, Indian Army

'A singular, valuable and admirable account of practising medicine during a time of war by the surgeon at the field hospital in Kargil. It was his first posting, and he was thrown into the deep end of things. *The Kargil War Surgeon's Testimony* makes for riveting reading.'

Nitin Gokhale, author of *Beyond NJ 9842: The Siachen Saga and R.N. Kao: The Gentleman Spymaster*

THE KARGIL WAR SURGEON'S TESTIMONY

Arup Ratan Basu

BLOOMSBURY
NEW DELHI • LONDON • OXFORD • NEW YORK • SYDNEY

*To all those soldiers who gave up their life and
youth, who fought till their last breath to protect
the honour and glory of our motherland*

BLOOMSBURY INDIA
Bloomsbury Publishing India Pvt. Ltd
Second Floor, LSC Building No. 4, DDA Complex, Pocket C – 6 & 7,
Vasant Kunj, New Delhi, 110070

BLOOMSBURY, BLOOMSBURY INDIA and the Diana logo
are trademarks of Bloomsbury Publishing Plc

First published in India 2025

Copyright © Arup Ratan Basu, 2025

Arup Ratan Basu has asserted his moral rights to be identified as the author
of this work in accordance with the Indian Copyright Act, 1957

Some names and details of individuals have been changed to preserve their
anonymity

All rights reserved. No part of this publication may be: i) reproduced or
transmitted in any form, electronic or mechanical, including photocopying,
recording or by means of any information storage or retrieval system without
prior permission in writing from the publishers; or ii) used or reproduced in
any way for the training, development or operation of artificial intelligence
(AI) technologies, including generative AI technologies. The rights holders
expressly reserve this publication from the text and data mining exception as
per Article 4(3) of the Digital Single Market Directive (EU) 2019/790

ISBN: PB: 978-93-61311-18-5; eBook: 978-93-61313-19-6

2 4 6 8 10 9 7 5 3 1

Typeset in Fournier MT Manipal Technologies Limited
Printed and bound in India by Thomson Press India Ltd

To find out more about our authors and books visit www.bloomsbury.com
and sign up for our newsletters

Author's Note

Kargil is a small town on the banks of the river Suru that flows through the Zanskar mountains in Kashmir. A conflict between India and Pakistan began brewing there in early May 1999. By the time I reached Kargil, the intensity of the conflict had increased and it was being called a 'localised warlike situation'. The Indian armed forces then launched a full-blown offensive, which was later named Operation Vijay. Thankfully, the situation did not escalate into a full-fledged war.

I had bought an ordinary hardbound notebook at the town bazaar to note my experiences during my stay in Kargil. In spite of the demands of my work, I managed to note the most important events of the time. Later, I completed the entries by filling in the details from memory. I finished writing the manuscript six months after returning home. The book you hold in your hands is that complete diary with all the events authentically described. I

Author's Note

have tried to write the book from a doctor's point of view, highlighting the human aspect of the conflict without going into the technical, logistic and strategic aspects of war.

In war, not all events are confirmed or even mentioned by the authorities. Many of the incidents and events you will find in this book may not have any official validation. I have, however, noted what people told me in confidence at the time, those who had come to me for treatment in the thick of battle. Some views are personal – I framed them after witnessing the conflict myself and then later developed them after leaving the warzone. These are tales that were heard or seen; in many instances, there is no proof or evidence to substantiate my statements. My story has to be taken at face value. It is my sincere hope that you will get a new perspective on the Kargil conflict of 1999 after reading this book.

While reading, do keep in mind that in 1999 there were no smartphones and very few people in India had mobile phones. Communication was still mostly dependent on letters and occasional long-distance phone calls, which were very expensive.

Author's Note

My account focuses on the human story of the war as experienced by a doctor. In this diary, I have included simple narrations of actual events and conversations. After the conflict ended, many reports and books were published on Operation Vijay. This book does not seek to compete with any of them. Neither should it be used as a weapon for political or bureaucratic gain.

I have tried to accord respect to the fallen soldiers of the Kargil conflict. Let us not perform a post-mortem of their deaths. We must remember that it is because of their martyrdom that our country is what it is today. We live because they sacrificed their lives.

I

The Suru and Its People

The sky was a shade of cobalt near the horizon and became a lighter hue at its zenith. Puffs of grey and white clouds wandered across the blue expanse, and the occasional bird chirped as it flew by. All around there were huge mountains, in different shades of dark brown or a deep ochre or dull grey. Some mountains were completely covered by a blanket of pearly white snow and ice.

These mountains existed long before humans ever walked this planet. They had no names but served as sentinels of the entire region. Now they are called the Himalaya, the Hindukush mountains and the Kunlun, Karakoram and Tien Shan ranges. The Himalaya were the source of life as they fed the rivers that coursed through the plains. It was by these rivers that great civilisations were established.

The Kargil War Surgeon's Testimony

Some rivers that emerge from the Himalaya are mighty, like the Ganga, while some others are less than a hundred kilometres long. But even these smaller rivers are essential for the survival of the people who live in the mountains. One such river is the Suru.

The Drang Drung glacier of the Zanskar region is the source of the Stod, the Tsarap and the Zanskar rivers, which are lifelines of the Padum and Zanskar valleys. There is another small stream of water that emanates from the north-western part of the glacier. It tumbles down the rocky slopes and flows below Panze-La, where it merges with the Parachik glacier. It then surges ahead through the rocky terrain of the Zanskar region, where water overflowing from the Nun and Kun peaks adds volume to the small river.

The river becomes livelier and swirls around the bends of the mountainous terrain, the clear and sparkling water tumbling down huge boulders and gushing down the slopes even as it is joined by other small rivulets that emerge from various crevices on the way. The locals call this river the Suru. Like a mother, the Suru nurtures life around itself as it passes through the barren, rocky landscapes. On either bank,

The Suru and Its People

the hustle and bustle of life emerges as crops of maize, wheat, barley and mustard thrive. Interspersed between the fields are apricot and walnut trees and the small houses of the shepherds and farmers who live there. The walls of the houses are made of stone and mud and the steep roofs of tin, slate and wood. Maize and barley are often laid out to dry on the roofs. Behind the huts are sheds with wooden pillars that house the sheep.

The river passes a monastery – called 'gompa' by the locals – known as Rangdum, where the monks start their day with a dip in its chilly waters. The monks then walk up the mountain in their crimson cloaks, rotating their prayer wheels in a clockwise direction while chanting 'Om Mani Padme Hum' and reciting their prayers. The monastery houses a huge wooden statue of the Maitreya deity sitting in the lotus position. The lives the monks and the local villagers lead seem to bring them closer to attaining the highest aspiration of the human race – peace of mind.

A narrow path along the river appears to be racing with the Suru, turning and bending until it crosses the river over a wooden bridge. The path then moves along the other bank before bidding farewell to the river and merging with a larger road. At this stage, the waters of the Suru are a turquoise blue mixed with occasional streaks of white froth. The surrounding fields are muddy brown with patches of light and dark moss.

The mountains around seem absolutely barren and lifeless. There is not a blade of grass on their rocky and sandy slopes, which are a shade of brownish yellow, dotted with orange and red rocks. The mountain slopes have been carved by the elements, with spots looking like abstract geometrical shapes or human figures. Looking closely, one might see an old man's bearded face or an old hunchback in the broken rocks. Before Rangdum gompa was established, monks had carved religious scriptures on to the sides of the mountains and even made some sculptures from the rocks there.

Along the Suru lies the small town of Kargil. It was an important trade centre on the Silk Route. For centuries the Suru has been peacefully flowing through the tranquil town. Today, the town is situated on the Leh–Srinagar highway and is an important tourist node for all visitors

The Suru and Its People

to the Zanskar region. Using Kargil as a base, travellers venture into the Zanskar mountains and Padum valley for hiking.

The residents of Kargil mostly work in the hotels and shops that cater to the requirements of the tourists. Most residents belong to the Shia sect of Islam, while others follow the Mahayana sect of Buddhism. As evening approaches, the shops bring down their shutters and the farmers and porters return home. The evenings are reserved for entertainment and prayers. Some indulge in gambling and drinking country liquor while others go for namaaz at the local mosque. The women seem to work more than the men. Besides housekeeping and rearing children, they also help with farming and running the family shop in the bazaar.

The bazaar has video parlours and counterfeit-goods shops. There one can find fake Cartier pens, Sony cameras and Levi Strauss jeans along with Belgian glassware and Chinese mink coats. The items all look genuine but are locally made. The tourists often frequent these shops.

The Suru flows through Kargil and then turns through a couple of gorges before merging into another river called the Shingo.

The Kargil War Surgeon's Testimony

The river respects no man-made borders and flows into the Gilgit area of northern Kashmir, which is under Pakistani control. The Suru eventually ends its journey by flowing into the mighty Indus.

There are many small towns and hamlets scattered in these mountains. Some of them are centuries old. The Indus river flows through some of these settlements, including Leh, Dah and Batalik. The residents of Dah are known as the Brokpas, and they speak the Brokskat language. For centuries they have maintained their cultural and physical isolation from the rest of the world. Until recently, it was forbidden for outsiders to venture near the village. It is believed that the villagers of Dah are descended from the lost soldiers of Alexander of Macedonia. They are tall with fair complexions and light-coloured eyes and wear bright, colourful dresses. In Dah, the residents have their own rituals, customs and beliefs, with most following a little-known animist religion.

The serenity of the Suru was rudely disrupted by the evil designs of an envious neighbour of

The Suru and Its People

India that had been trying desperately to get control over the entire region through whatever means it could. For many years, Pakistan had been disregarding previous pacts with India, waging proxy wars and sponsoring terror attacks in India. In 1999, they again changed strategy and infiltrated the border, destroying the peaceful life of the Kargil valley.

The town of Kargil and the road connecting it to Leh and Srinagar were heavily bombarded by artillery shells from across the border. The big guns shattered the silence of the valley and shook the mountains from their bases. Life came to a standstill as the terrified people of the valley left their homes, perhaps never to return.

The Suru flowed on through it all, even as its land and the people there faced an uncertain future.

2

Journey into the Valley

It was December 1998, and I had just qualified as a surgeon in the Indian Army Medical Corps after three years of toiling through case sheets, surgeries and night shifts while being reprimanded by teachers and seniors. Finally, the stresses of finishing my thesis and clearing the post-graduation examinations were behind me. My fellow graduates and I were expecting to get assigned to various hospitals around the country. There, we would get to hone our skills under a senior surgeon and then serve as independent surgeons.

I received my posting as a surgeon in a field hospital in the Kashmir valley. My unit was located in a hotspot of militant activity. At first, I wondered if I would be tending to casualties in addition to the routine cases, but I soon found out that the field hospital was not equipped with a functional operation theatre. I was surprised.

Journey into the Valley

Why was I getting posted there? Surely there had been a mistake, and they had thought that I was a general practitioner. Soon, my feelings changed to anger.

I was frustrated to see my friends packing their bags and leaving to take up their postings in major cities such as Agra, Ahmedabad, Kolkata and Pune. They were moving to established hospitals and would get relevant workloads. Two years at a place without any surgical work would mark the end of my career as a surgeon before it had even begun. Why me, I wondered? What had I done to deserve this?

No one could answer my questions. Though some of my friends offered their sympathies and tried to console me, I felt miserable. I walked around the wards of the hospital with a dry smile pasted on my face to hide my sorrow even as I made preparations to move to Kashmir.

Kashmir is called the Switzerland of India. But when I headed there, it was February and the peak of winter – a time when the valley was at its dullest. My mood was similar to the bleak surroundings as the army convoy I was travelling in entered the valley through the Jawahar tunnel. My journey had commenced from a Jammu transit camp in a convoy comprising over thirty vehicles – mainly buses and trucks but also some cars. We were accompanied by armed Jeeps for protection. I was assigned a seat on the officers' bus. The plan was to stop for lunch at Banihal and reach Srinagar by evening.

As we emerged from the Jawahar tunnel, I could see nothing extraordinary about the place we were in. Was this the so-called Paradise on Earth? It just looked cold, desolate and lifeless to me. The sky was overcast, and the road was covered in snow. Even seeing snow did not excite me at all in my cynical state. In the distance, mountain ranges ran parallel to the road, which passed through seemingly endless stretches of dry brown fields. The trees lining the road were barren. There was not a single flower to be seen anywhere. I could not recognise the trees as they were quite different from the ones I knew or had seen before. A fellow passenger on the bus told me that they were chinars.

Every now and then we passed a village or a small town. The air around those settlements was smoky. The smoke was from the chimneys of the bukharis, large ovens that run on coal or wood. The bukhari was placed in a room at

Journey into the Valley

the centre of the house and people sat around it, usually on the floor. That one room was the only heated room in the house and was the centre of all domestic activities.

In some villages, I noticed a few large houses in a state of disrepair. Their walls had crumbled and roofs had blown off. I guessed they were probably the houses of the Hindu pandits who had to suddenly leave their homes and escape from the Kashmir valley when intense militant activity had started in the region in the late 1980s. Those who had tried to stay on were either killed or had their houses blown up by the militants. I reflected on those sad days and wondered whether the original inhabitants of those houses could ever come back to their village and their land.

After some time, we passed a market. The shopkeepers were dressed in the long, loose overcoat known as 'firan'. Some of the menfolk huddled in front of the shops and shared a hukkah as the shopkeepers chatted with them while attending to their customers. Among the wares were walnuts, apricots and almonds. The women wore colourful firans, with intricate embroidery on the front. Some of them had huge protruding bellies. It struck me as odd that so many women could be pregnant at the same time until I realised that they had concealed kangris – earthen pots filled with burning charcoal – under their firans to keep themselves warm!

Some villagers stared at the passing military vehicles with suspicion clear on their faces. Their eyes seemed to reflect their inner despair and hopelessness. Why were they looking at us as if we were unwelcome strangers? What exactly were they thinking? Perhaps they were wondering if we had come as friends to help them or if we were the enemy. I decided not to bother myself with it. Personnel of the Indian armed forces should not get involved with the local politics of the areas they serve.

A few elderly men were sitting under a huge chinar tree. Their expressions and demeanour were different from that of the rest of the villagers. They displayed a look of gratitude as they waved at us and saluted our convoy. Some of them were even smiling. I wondered if they were retired military or security personnel – or were they simply pragmatic enough to fathom that without the Indian armed forces present their land would be totally overrun by the Pakistani Army and militants, as it had been in October 1947.

Journey into the Valley

Our convoy passed Khanabal, Anantnag and Avantipur. On either side of the road were shrubs with dried violet flowers as far as the eye could see. These were the famous saffron crops of the region. 'Saffron is very expensive,' said the person sitting next to me. 'Just ten grams will set you back a few hundred rupees. The locals over here believe that if a pregnant woman has saffron with milk, she will be blessed with a fair-complexioned child. But be careful when buying it, because a lot of imitation products are on sale around here.'

The traffic increased as we approached Srinagar. It was the main hub of the Kashmir valley for both civilians and the military. Our convoy moved slowly. The buildings were bigger and the crowd denser. On both sides of the road were huge chinar trees. The trees had five-pointed star-shaped leaves, which are a symbol of the Kashmir valley. Soon, we turned into the high-security area that was the Srinagar transit camp. Due to the large number of military personnel present, the camp was an obvious high-value target for the militants. This meant that the area was heavily fortified, and gruelling guard duty was demanded of the soldiers around the clock.

The Kargil War Surgeon's Testimony

The river Jhelum flowed along on one side of the camp, while the snow-clad mountains of Gulmarg could be seen in the distance. Inside, there was a beautiful garden near the mess area. But I did not have the inclination to appreciate such beauty in that highly tense and hostile atmosphere. The chaos of the officers' transit camp was managed by a person called Shukla-ji. He was the jack-of-all-trades of the Srinagar transit camp.

The next day, I was taken to a place called Pattan, which was approximately twenty kilometres before Baramulla. The area is famed for the 'Golden Delicious' variety of apple, considered the best in the Kashmir valley. It was also notorious for the highest militant activity in the region. That was where I was to be stationed – in the middle of an apple orchard that the army had leased.

As expected, there was no operation theatre there. I understood that I was to serve as reserve surgeon, stepping in whenever the main surgeon was absent. Sometimes, I had to travel north to places such as Handwara, Kupwara, Nyari and Chowkibal. Eventually, I went to a field hospital at Tangdhar in the Karnah valley, quite close to the Line of Control, where I spent three weeks working as an independent surgeon. It felt good to be back in touch with surgery and brush away the cobwebs from my fingers. I hoped to get more surgical work in the future.

3
Shaktiman with Wings

Back in Pattan, I whiled away my time taking long walks through the apple orchards during my free time and playing badminton in the evening. During the day, there were some hospital duties and non-surgical patient management. One evening, we heard that some twenty-odd militants had crossed the Line of Control into Indian territory somewhere in the mountains. They were suspected to be Taliban militants, but no one was sure what their objective was. However, the feeling was that they would soon be wiped out by the Indian Army.

A couple of days later, I received instructions to move to Kargil. I had heard of it before and already knew that it was a small town by the Suru in the Zanskar range. It was at an elevation of approximately 9,200 feet above sea level, with winter temperatures dropping as low as minus 20 degrees Celsius. From Srinagar, one had to drive through Sonmarg, Zoji La and Dras to reach Kargil. The road then continued on to Lamayuru and Nimu before ending at Leh. It was also possible to fly to Leh using either commercial or military aircraft and then travel from Leh to Kargil by road.

I asked the adjutant of my unit when I was supposed to leave and was told that I had to be in Kargil as soon as possible, because the surgeon over there was to go on leave for two months. 'He should be leaving in a week or so,' said the adjutant. I asked him how big the hospital was. I wanted to know about the workload.

'There is a smallish field hospital,' said the officer. 'I think it is less than fifty beds. I think there is only one brigade there, and maybe an infantry unit. The work there is quite relaxed, from what I've heard from your predecessors.' He said there might be a surgery every other day, and the rest of the time could be spent in leisure activities and feasting on the region's famed khurmani, or apricots as we call them. However, I wished for a busier schedule.

It was the second week of May 1999 when I found myself back at the Srinagar transit camp, trying to figure out a way to reach Kargil. The camp seemed much more chaotic, and the officers' mess area was full of women and children, with the younger ones crying listlessly. They appeared to be the families of officers who were not present. There was uncertainty in the air. Officers with stern, tense faces were pacing around. I wondered what was going on and walked over to Shukla-ji at the reception counter to find out.

'I don't know the specifics, sir, but something has happened in the higher mountains,' he told me. 'The wives and children of officers are being asked to leave the area and troop movement has suddenly increased. They are all moving north.'

I told him that I had to go to Kargil and asked what I should do.

'Kargil, sir? That is where the trouble is.' He then gave me the standard military advice: '*Aap dekh lo, sir* [You have to see to it for yourself, sir].'

That meant I had to make my own arrangements and reach Kargil through any means available. Around me, the huge Shaktiman trucks were heading out of the transit camp in convoys. They were headed towards

Sonmarg and would probably go on to Kargil. I noticed that some of the trucks were carrying the big Bofors artillery guns. I decided to see if I could hitch a ride on one of those trucks.

A short walk outside the transit camp took me to a large area called the convoy ground, where all convoy vehicles assembled before setting out. The place was buzzing with military personnel. I was confident that no militant attack would happen there. All around me troops were rushing about, and the convoy commanders were trying to sort out the chaos.

However, I could not find any officers to talk to about my situation. I asked a few people here and there, but no one appeared to want to take me along. While I was walking around the convoy ground, it struck me that the road from Dras to Kargil was a dangerous one. There was heavy shelling on that road from across the border. What if a shell hit the vehicle I was in? That would be the end of this story before it had even begun.

I gave up trying to travel to Kargil by road and walked over to the nearby helipad. It was small, probably a makeshift one. But when I asked an officer if he could fly me to Kargil, he gave me a cold look.

'Are you out of your mind?' he shouted. 'Even brigadiers and generals are having a tough time arranging a h'eptr for themselves!' I knew from my military training lessons that the term h'eptr was the shortening of 'helicopter' that many in the army used. But there was to be no h'eptr for me.

There was one option left. Every Monday, an air force courier aircraft transported military personnel from Srinagar to Chandigarh. The soldiers and officers who were going on leave could reach Chandigarh in an hour. *Luckily*, I thought, *it is a Sunday, so I can take that flight tomorrow*. I registered for the flight and arrived well before time at the airport.

After waiting for over three hours past the scheduled departure, I was told that though the flight was quite popular, it was not very regular. It would sometimes arrive a day late. That is what happened that day. Some technical snag meant that the plane would not arrive that day, and we were told to come back to the airport the next morning.

The next day, the huge aircraft did arrive, and an hour later, we were at Chandigarh airfield. I went to the Chandigarh transit camp, which was close to the airfield, to make further

Shaktiman with Wings

arrangements for my travel. Chandigarh is the most important air force station in the northern sector with air connectivity to Leh, Thoise and Srinagar. The aircraft of the Indian Air Force were lifelines for the soldiers at the forward locations. The best and the shortest way to proceed to a destination in the northern sector was on an air force plane. There were daily flights to Leh, and I made arrangements to be on the next day's flight. I could then proceed to Kargil from Leh.

I was back at the airfield at 5 a.m. the next day. The aircraft was a Russian-made IL-76, a huge aircraft capable of carrying over two hundred passengers. However, it was mainly used to transport cargo, so the seats were collapsible wooden ones built into the sides, with the rest of the interior a huge metallic cavern with wires, pulleys, levers, rollers, cranks and trolley ramps on the roof and the floor. The IL-76 was aptly nicknamed 'Shaktiman with wings'.

Between the two rows of seats was the cargo, which included ammunition, military supplies, foodstuff, mail, machinery and the luggage of the passengers. The cargo was covered by a huge tarpaulin sheet secured with strong ropes. On top of the tarpaulin sheet were a dozen jawans who had not managed to secure a seat. Because they had to report to their duty station as soon as possible, they had boarded the plane regardless and travelled holding on to the ropes in lieu of seat belts.

Fifty minutes later, we landed at Leh. I complimented the pilot on the landing as I disembarked.

'Thank you, Major,' he responded. 'Where are you off to?'

'Kargil, sir.'

'Uh-oh, Kargil? Well, all the best.'

I asked him if there were any problems there. He told me that there was a lot of serious action happening at that place now as about a hundred militants were suspected to have crossed over the Line of Control.

A whiff of cold air greeted me as I walked out of the aircraft carrying my suitcase. It was about 8 a.m. The airfield was in a flat area of dry and arid soil and all around were barren mountains. It was as though I was standing on an alien planet. The cold and silent mountains appeared to be sentinels guarding the Leh valley, protecting the civilisations that have existed in this region over the centuries.

Shaktiman with Wings

I noticed a monastery in the distance. Scattered all around the place were buildings whose colours were quite similar to that of the mountains, making them appear camouflaged. Down below, in the valley, was a small river that seemed to me like a worm twisting and turning as it crawled forward. I presumed it was the Indus. There was an eerie silence there, broken only by the sound of the strong breeze whistling through the valley and the occasional rumbling of military trucks.

As I walked in that silence, I felt a bit breathless. I slowed my pace and thought about what the pilot had said. What exactly was the matter at Kargil?

4
A Way to Kargil

I had to find a way to Kargil, but there was no one I knew at Leh. I decided that the safest place to halt was the transit camp outside Leh. It was on the road to Kargil. After a wash and a quick breakfast, I made enquiries and was informed that a Jeep was heading to Kargil shortly. A white Maruti Gypsy of the Intelligence Corps pulled over, and I was offered the front seat. I thought it was a stroke of luck, as it would have taken me two days to get to Kargil in the army convoy. We headed out on the National Highway 1A, the road that would eventually reach Srinagar via Zoji La.

At places, we drove along the river Indus. The water was like a mirror reflecting the mountains and the sky. The road then left the river and climbed for a while. I spotted another small monastery in the mountains. Around the gompa were small houses. I assumed that was

A Way to Kargil

where the monks lived. We passed a group of cute, pink-cheeked children carrying big bags as they reluctantly walked to school. Their school uniforms looked out of place in these surroundings. I wondered why modern education required small children to carry such heavy loads to and from school. For centuries, this area had been isolated from the rest of the world. The people of this land had developed a civilisation and culture of their own, but now they were in danger of losing their original identity. The youth of this region were already adopting a more modern lifestyle and leaving behind traditional society. I wondered if the traditions of this land would survive the test of time. Would that gompa still be there a few years from now?

The highway passed through a completely barren and isolated stretch of land that had no signs of civilisation or life. The area all around was rocky and sandy, the undulating landscape a dull yellow. There was not a single bird in the sky. It looked very similar to pictures of the Martian landscape, with the highway a black worm inching forward towards infinity.

We passed a gurdwara called Pathar Sahib. The Sikhs believe that when Guru Nanak had rested at this site, a demon had hurled a rock at him. Guru Nanak had stopped the rock with his hands and feet. The marks of his hands and feet were imprinted on the rock. A gurdwara was built at the location.

The driver of the Gypsy decided to kill the monotony of the journey by playing some music. However, due to a defect in the car's music system, the cassette played at an irregular speed. Instead of music what came out was a jumbled cacophony. However, the driver was determined to enjoy the 'music' and the same cassette was played on repeat for the rest of the journey.

Down below in the gorge, the Indus – which was called 'Sindhu' by the locals – was much stronger and mightier than it had been in Leh. It was turbulent and crashing angrily over the rocks, twisting and turning at the bends. I saw another river merging with the Indus. It was the Zanskar, its light-green waters blending with the muddy grey of the Indus.

We passed a small hamlet called Nimu. The river was broader and slower there, with more greenery around. I noticed stacks of hay and wheat piled by the side of the road. There were also square blocks of stone with conical tops. These were called 'chortens' – ancient tombstones of lamas. Many of them looked centuries old and some were crumbling to dust.

Suddenly, the driver stopped the car, switched off the engine and shifted the gear to neutral. Half a minute later, the car slowly started moving by itself. It was perfectly level ground there, so how was the car moving? I wondered. The driver told me that somewhere in the mountains to our right was a huge magnet that pulled the car and made it move. Was I imagining things?

The journey continued through the Zanskar mountains. To our right was the mighty Karakoram range, where the Siachen glacier was located. It also had the famous Karakoram Pass, which travellers on the medieval Silk Route traversed on their way to Ladakh. Somewhere in the distance straight ahead was the spot where the Karakoram, Hindu Kush and Hindu Raj mountain ranges met the Himalaya. It is called the Pamir Knot. On the map the ranges look so small, but it is upon seeing them that one appreciates their imposing presence.

We drove through the bleak, desolate landscape, with the jarring and monotonous music playing in our car continuously, before eventually stopping for lunch at a place called

Khalsi. It is a small town located on the banks of the Indus, from where a narrow road diverges towards Batalik and the Line of Control. The river turns away towards Dah here. It flows onward to the Gilgit and Baltistan regions of Pakistan-occupied Kashmir on the other side of the Line of Control. Rivers and mountains respect no man-made borders and don't bother with visas and passports.

The road curved along hairpin bends as it began to climb. My head started spinning like a top, and at every turn I felt that the car would slip off the road and tumble into the gorge. However, the driver skilfully manoeuvred the vehicle and after an hour we had ascended to a height of about 13,000 feet above sea level. When we came to a halt, I stepped out of the car and gazed at the barren valley below.

It was a bird's-eye view, the road appearing as a piece of thread fallen over the mountains. I noticed other army vehicles on the road. Even the big Shaktimans looked like ants. The driver told me that the road was nicknamed 'Jalebi Mor'. An appropriate name for such a twisty, loopy route, I thought.

The next town we drove through was Lamayuru. At a little distance from the main town, there was a gompa with a shear vertical wall perched on top of a hill. It looked quite inaccessible and was probably built there so that the monks could meditate without being disturbed. The Lamayuru monastery looked very familiar to me and I couldn't understand why until I remembered seeing a similar-looking building in the comic *Tintin in Tibet*.

We drove through a mountain pass and then the road started a descent. Behind a gompa we passed was a 20-foot-high statue of Maitreya – or the 'future Buddha' – carved out of a single block of rock. I learned that the statue was carved sometime in the first century BCE.

As we neared Kargil, the landscape started to change. There were a few shrubs on the mountains and occasionally a few trees on the side of the road. Down in the valley I saw a small rivulet. It was the Suru. Fields of dry grass and wheat appeared on the riverbank. No sooner had we entered the Kargil valley than we encountered an army sentry post. Our Jeep came to a halt.

It was around 4 p.m. We had arrived. A soldier approached our car. Our driver casually asked him, 'What is the situation now?'

'They were firing some time back,' replied the jawan. 'One of their shells fell over there, near that rock. It almost hit a school building, but no one was hurt.'

The driver asked if we should continue onward.

'There has been no shelling for some time. Hopefully they will not fire again today. You can go ahead.'

I did not like the conversation one bit. They were talking about gunfire from the enemy in such a cool and calm manner! It amazed me. And then it struck me that I was headed to a place where shelling occurred regularly. Good Lord! I thought. All I can do is keep a cool head and focus on my work, I told myself. Like the song 'Que Sera, Sera' goes, whatever will be, will be.

5

The Small Field Hospital

At about 4.30 p.m. on 19 May 1999, I reached the officers' mess of the Kargil Field Ambulance. I was relieving the duties of the surgeon on duty, Major R.P.S. Gambhir. He was mighty glad to see me and asked me to make myself comfortable in his room. Then he immediately started packing his bags so that he could leave the very next day. I was to remain in this place for the next two months, serving as the sole surgeon until Major Gambhir returned.

I only had one month of surgical experience, and I had passed my postgraduate exams just four months ago. I wondered whether I would be able to perform what was required of me – especially the management of war casualties. I was a bit apprehensive but I reminded myself that fear was equivalent to death, an idea made popular by the villain Gabbar in the movie *Sholay*: *'Jo darr gaya samjho mar gaya!'*

The Kargil War Surgeon's Testimony

The road going down to the field hospital descended further down and crossed the Suru over a small steel bridge. That was the link that connected this place to the Leh–Srinagar highway. Turning right on the road beyond the bridge would take one past the town of Kargil and onward to Dras and Srinagar. Turning left, one could proceed to Minjee and then on to a place called Padum, high in the Zanskar range.

Major Gambhir's room – soon to be mine – was small, with thick tin sheets serving as the roof over a false ceiling made of compact board. In one corner of the roof was a jagged hole through which the sky was visible. I asked Major Gambhir about it. He smiled and told me not to worry. Then he pointed to a corner of the room. My gaze followed his finger and saw a partially crushed wooden bed. The wood appeared burnt at some places. There was a large fragment of an artillery shell by it.

'Come on,' beckoned Major Gambhir. I followed him outside. He pointed to the hill opposite us. On the slopes high above us I could see a blackish patch of soil with pieces of something embedded in it.

'That burnt patch over there was the ammunition dump of Kargil,' said the major.

The Small Field Hospital

'On 9 May, there was intense shelling around here. Several shells landed on that hill, with some falling close to our hospital. Then one shell hit the ammunition dump, setting it ablaze. It was a terrible sight – massive explosions with all kinds of ammunition bursting and flying everywhere.' The fire, he said, lasted for almost a day. That was when a fragment of an exploded shell came flying and hit the roof of his room. It tore open a hole and fell inside. 'Luckily, I was in the operation theatre then,' said Major Gambhir. 'The bed caught fire, though.'

He sounded pretty relaxed about the entire episode. 'And the strangest thing,' he continued, 'during the shelling there were four soldiers hiding in a bunker under the ammo dump. After the fire subsided, the rescue team went in search of their remains. And guess what? All four of them walked out. They had survived despite being right under an exploding ammo dump for a day. As they say, if God is with you, even the devil cannot get you!'

I was speechless. After regaining my composure, I said, 'And you continued to sleep in that room? Did you not think of changing to another room? I'm supposed to stay here for the next two months ... what if another shell lands in that room?'

'It won't,' said the major confidently. 'Lightning doesn't strike the same place twice. Just relax.'

Another thought struck me. 'That side of the hill is exposed to the enemy, so any Pakistani shell flying across those hills could have hit the dump,' I said. 'How come no one thought about that? Why did they not shift the ammunition dump to a safer place when the trouble was first noticed?'

The major smiled again. 'That was one of the first thoughts that had come up,' he said. 'The case report was made and forwarded to the authorities in Delhi.'

'Then why was no action taken?'

'No one knows. Probably some hitch somewhere. But the result was that precious ammunition was lost at a time when trouble started pouring in.'

We walked back to the officers' mess, where I was introduced to the commanding officer and the second-in-command. I also met Major Ramprasad, the anaesthesiologist; Captain Sunil, the medical officer and Major Anupama, who was in charge of casualty and the only

The Small Field Hospital

female doctor present. There was also Captain Sugumar, who was the quartermaster – an administrative position in a field hospital.

I noticed that some of the families of the officers were present. The wives had come over to spend some time with their husbands and brought along the children as well, because they were on their summer vacations. I learned that this was the norm in Kargil during the summer months. However, this year everything seemed topsy-turvy, and the families weren't sure how long they could stay there, nor how they would make their journey back home.

The officers were speaking about places where units were getting deployed. I heard names such as Kaksar, Dras, Tololing, Tiger Hill, Mushkoh, Bajrang and Kukarthang. Except for Dras, I had not heard of any of these places. Captain Sugumar was talking about the Bofors gun being deployed at Apathe, but I had no idea where Apathe was. Seeing my perplexed expression, Major Ramprasad explained that most of these places were located close to the Line of Control. Our soldiers were being deployed there to prevent the intrusion of militants.

The Kargil War Surgeon's Testimony

'What exactly is going on here, man?' I asked Major Ramprasad.

'We don't know exactly,' he admitted. 'But there's some serious problem at the heights along the Line of Control. Every day at sundown, we are receiving ten to twelve casualties. They are mostly sepoys, lance naiks and naiks, and nearly all of them have splinter or bullet wounds. Some are quite serious.'

He went on to explain that after being stabilised with intravenous fluids, they were operated on through the night. The next day, if they were stable enough, they were sent to the hospital at Leh – or to Srinagar if a helicopter was available.

'We cannot keep them here for long as we have only forty-nine beds,' explained Ramprasad. 'Some beds have to be kept open for medical emergencies, so we have to evacuate the minor casualties every other day.'

'What kind of surgeries are being done here?' I asked.

'All kinds ... removal of splinters from the limbs and sealing of the wounds, especially those in the abdomen and chest. Basically, we have to stabilise the casualty first and control the spread of infection. Then we try to close the

The Small Field Hospital

wound and make him as pain-free as possible. After that, they have to go off.'

I gulped upon hearing this. It was apparent that they were doing all kinds of surgeries here in this small field hospital, with such limited facilities. I was again anxious about my very limited experience. Major Gambhir noticed my expression and patted me on the back.

'Don't worry,' he said. 'Just do whatever you've learned. All will be good. Don't be afraid or you're finished!'

I asked if this was a temporary state of affairs or if it would take long to deal with the hundred-odd militants who had infiltrated.

'No, it seems the number is much more,' said the major. 'They may not just be militants either, as they seem to be well equipped and prepared to carry out a long-term offensive. It's quite likely that regulars of the Pakistani Army are present at the heights. They have probably only sent in a few hundred so far. We don't feel that it is a matter that will die out soon. We all hope that it does, though.'

'What are they planning to do in this remote, desolate area?'

'As per the brigade briefing I attended, their first objective is to capture the heights along

The Kargil War Surgeon's Testimony

the Line of Control in this area. As you know, whoever captures the heights in mountainous terrain has the upper hand. From there they could bombard the Srinagar–Leh highway and also towns such as Kargil and Dras. That would cut off the convoys to Leh and ultimately result in the Siachen glacier falling in enemy hands. Then this route would become an easy entry point for other militants.'

Major Gambhir went on to explain that the Line of Control to the north of us is loosely demarcated, often running across heights at about 14,000 to 15,000 feet. Towards the east, it reaches 17,000 to 19,000 feet, and that is where the Siachen glacier is. The region receives very heavy snow through the winter months. Apart from the glacier, which is permanently frozen, the snow and ice don't start to melt until about May. Because of this, India and Pakistan have a pact that the region of the Line of Control would work under the system of 'winter-vacated posts'. This meant that there would be no troops at the Line of Control over the winter at that height. The last patrolling ends by November and resumes the following May, once the snow starts to melt.

The Small Field Hospital

'This year, though we had vacated the posts as per the pact, it appears that they had not,' said the major. 'Or perhaps they had but then returned to reoccupy them. And now they are well positioned to target us. This is what we presume, of course.'

I was left wondering why we are always betrayed by our neighbours. In the three wars that we have fought with Pakistan, they were forced to surrender each time and had to agree to peace pacts. Then they always went back on their word and started the same thing again. Why do they have so much hatred for India? Why don't they develop themselves instead of fighting with us?

Captain Sugumar revealed that there was an Intelligence Corps officer who occasionally dined with them at the mess. They received all their updates from him. According to that officer, the first sighting of the intruders was by the Bakarwals, the local shepherds who graze their sheep and yak on the mountain slopes. They had gone to the heights once the snow had begun to melt in the first week of May. That was when they had seen some men in black outfits digging a bunker at those heights. This was in the Batalik sector. On

The Kargil War Surgeon's Testimony

receiving this intelligence, the army had sent a team of six soldiers headed by Captain Saurav Kalia for a patrol. That was on 15 May. However, there had been no news from them since.

I was shocked to hear that. 'Do you mean that they are missing?'

The quartermaster confirmed that to be true and added that more troops were sent after that. 'That was when casualties started arriving here every day,' he finished.

I was bewildered. The situation was worse than I had imagined.

'What will happen?' I asked. 'Are we moving towards war?'

'I don't know, sir. But whatever it is, it had better end soon … otherwise …'

Captain Sugumar didn't finish. I was shocked out of my wits. This was supposed to be just a temporary posting with one-off surgeries and time spent taking long walks and eating apricots. The sun was on its way down as we sipped our tea in our combat uniforms, talking casually about an outbreak of war.

'Anyway, we just have to carry on with our work,' said the quartermaster. 'In our corps we always work throughout the year, don't

The Small Field Hospital

we? Right now, we are working a bit more – that's all.'

He pointed at a particular hillslope that was more prone to shelling as it was facing the enemy side. Our hospital was on the opposite slope, he said, so the shelling was comparatively infrequent there. 'But yes, we do receive shelling once in a while,' said the captain. 'Nothing we can do about it, is there?'

Major Gambhir spoke up. 'Artillery fire and shelling started from the first week of May this year,' he said. 'It used to occasionally happen near the Dras highway but not here. What we have learned over the past two weeks is that when shelling occurs, if you hear a dull thud in front of you when facing north, it is probably Pakistani fire. But if you see a flash of light and hear a booming noise to your right, it is the gun of our artillery. Now listen very carefully. If you hear a screeching sound just after the dull thud in front of you, it is a Pakistani artillery shell flying overhead. It would have already crossed us. However, if you do not hear a screeching sound after the thud in the north, then it is one of two things: The shell may be heading towards a totally different direction. Or ... the shell may be heading straight towards us. It'll hit us before we can hear the screeching sound.'

My eyes almost popped out of their sockets. Major Gambhir seemed so unperturbed as he casually told me this. It was dark by then. He looked at his watch. 'Strange,' he said. 'I thought it was time.'

Time, I wondered? Time for what?

6

The First Night

It was then that the telephone rang. A havildar received the call and came over to us. 'Sir, there are casualties coming,' he announced. 'Twelve of them.' Major Gambhir and Major Ramprasad stood up. 'Let's go,' Major Gambhir said to me. 'It's time.'

We walked to the hospital. It took us about ten minutes. A couple of minutes after we arrived, two one-ton Nissan trucks and an ambulance arrived with casualties from the Dras sector. Major Gambhir instructed me to stand to one side and watch the proceedings. I did as he asked. The wounded soldiers were wheeled in one after another. Some of them were groaning in pain, while others were relatively silent.

The hospital staff started working quickly and efficiently with no fuss, each one knowing what to do and when to do it. The casualties were disrobed by the nursing assistants and housekeeper and their uniforms placed in a corner. Their particulars were noted by another orderly and the registration of their documentation was done. Then their injuries were examined by Major Gambhir and the case sheets written quickly yet neatly by Major Anupama.

After the examination, the patients were accorded priority as per the seriousness of their condition. This process is known as 'triage'. Basic resuscitation with intravenous fluids was started and X-rays of the injured area were taken by a portable X-ray machine that had been brought to the ward from the radiology room. Antibiotics were administered and the operation theatre was instructed to prepare for surgery.

'Let's go,' Major Gambhir said to me. 'Anupama will look after them for now.'

'Sir, what about the surgeries?' I asked.

'Plenty of time for that. Let them be stabilised first. Let's get dinner in the meantime.'

We rushed to the mess for a quick and early dinner. Fifteen minutes later, we were back at the hospital. As per priority, the first case was already in the operation theatre. The other patients were waiting in the ward.

The First Night

I noted the various types of injuries the soldiers had. They were mostly wounds from bullets or from splinters of artillery shells. One patient had a partially avulsed chest wall – the skin and muscles over the right side of his chest had been ripped away by a large splinter from an artillery shell. Others had splinters in their limbs, necks and shoulders.

Major Gambhir explained to me that splinters, or shrapnel, are the remnants of an exploded artillery shell. These hot, jagged pieces of metal – weighing anywhere from a few grams to a few kilos – become deadly missiles with uneven, sharp edges that travel as fast as bullets whenever a shell explodes. Because of their irregular shapes they cause much more damage than a bullet.

'They can travel anywhere in the body by their own spin, yaw and tumble,' said Major Gambhir. 'Do you remember the chapter on war wounds and kinetic energy in Bailey and Love's *Short Practice of Surgery*? Well, the movement of a splinter is not mentioned there. It can move in any way that you can imagine!'

The casualties requiring surgery were operated on one after the other. They were brought in turn to the operation theatre and

The Kargil War Surgeon's Testimony

then led away as if at an assembly line in a factory. Instruments were changed, replaced and sterilised. Even the assistants changed, but Major Gambhir and Major Ramprasad constantly stood at the operation table.

'I think I should scrub up, sir,' I said, offering to help.

'No need,' replied Major Gambhir. 'I can manage. Don't worry, you'll have enough on your plate from tomorrow.'

I continued to watch. Sometime later, he said, 'You've been travelling for three days. Go and rest and prepare for tomorrow.'

Heeding Major Gambhir's instructions, I walked back to my room. It was 3 a.m., and the area was pitch dark. An eerie silence reigned. It seemed life only existed back at the field hospital.

The next day, I saw Major Gambhir returning from the hospital as I was leaving my room for the day. He had performed surgeries through the night without respite and now would take an hour's rest before returning to arrange for the safe evacuation of the casualties to a bigger hospital in Leh or Srinagar. Later in the day, Major Gambhir would leave for his vacation. I was taking

The First Night

over his responsibilities and would have to do all that I saw him do the previous day.

I moved my luggage to his room wondering all the while how I could step into an experienced surgeon's boots. Could I manage everything that was expected of me? I was going to sleep in a room with a hole in the roof that served as a reminder that anything could happen at any time. I remembered Major Gambhir's statement: 'Lightning does not strike the same place twice.' And then I confidently entered the room.

7

A Proper Reception

We did not have a wide choice of channels to watch on television – it was only Doordarshan and Zee News. That is what we were watching after lunch the next day when Major Ramprasad suddenly said, 'It has been almost two days since you have arrived, and you have not received a proper reception here.' I was wondering what he was talking about when there was a terrible booming noise outside and the building shook.

We rushed outside and I understood what Major Ramprasad meant by 'proper reception'. Smoke was billowing from behind some trees on the other side of the river. It was a Pakistani artillery shell, landing barely a kilometre from us. I was reminded of the saying that as soon as someone joins the army, a bullet or artillery shell is made with his name on it.

A Proper Reception

The telephone rang two minutes later.

'Sir, the convoy halting area has been hit,' said the person calling. 'I will call again shortly.'

Five minutes later, the phone rang again.

'Sir, casualties are on their way to the field ambulance.'

'How many?' asked Major Ramprasad.

'Eleven, sir.'

The anaesthetist and I set off for the hospital. My surgical tenure at Kargil was about to start. The casualties arrived and were assessed and stabilised. Everything happened exactly as I had observed yesterday. No one changed the drill and no questions were asked. Everyone worked with silent efficiency. I proceeded to the operation theatre.

The first case was a twenty-one-year-old sepoy. A small splinter had penetrated his left armpit. He was conscious and there was just a trickle of blood in his armpit. Something told me that there was more to it than met the eye. Indeed, as soon as we started to clean the wound, there was a sudden gush of blood from it. The splinter had probably severed the axillary artery or one of its branches. Within half a minute, the patient's blood pressure collapsed.

The Kargil War Surgeon's Testimony

Major Ramprasad yelled at me to do something. I began with some local anaesthesia and made an incision. In the meantime, Major Ramprasad started general anaesthesia and set up the intravenous fluids. There was blood everywhere, and my mind was galloping. The axillary artery and its branches, the vein, the brachial plexus and all its branches and nodes – the anatomy I had studied – all flashed in front of my eyes. I remembered that the axillary artery is the main artery supplying the arm, while the brachial plexus is the network of nerves supplying the upper part of the limb. One wrong move could spell disaster, and a delay could mean death.

I started with the time-tested techniques of surgery. After compressing the area with warm saline-soaked swabs, I kept the suction ready and had my assistant hand over the artery forceps. I reminded myself to adjust the light and not to panic. After a minute of compression, I ventured into the axilla while slowly removing the swab. The blood was now flowing at a slower pace, and the anatomy was clearer. I could identify the bleeders – it was an anterior branch of the axillary artery and a vein. I used the artery forceps to apply

A Proper Reception

firm ligatures and brought the situation under control.

Phew, what a start, I thought as I heaved a sigh of relief. The entire operation took only fifteen minutes, but it seemed like a very long time. As we were rechecking the operated area, a soft voice spoke from over my shoulder.

'May I see it please, if you don't mind?'

I turned to find an elderly gentleman of medium build. He seemed to be a native of the area. Major Ramprasad quickly said, 'This is Dr Kachu Hussain, a very experienced local surgeon. I called him. Thankfully, he was around and has come to help out.'

I stepped aside and let Dr Kachu examine my work.

'Yes, it looks fine,' he said after a moment. 'I think it can be closed.'

We took a breather and had some tea while the operation theatre was cleaned and the next patient was wheeled in. I took the opportunity to get acquainted with Dr Kachu. He was a general surgeon who had been practising at the district hospital for the past twenty years. He seemed to be a quiet man with the typical facial features of

The Kargil War Surgeon's Testimony

a Ladakh native. Though he was supposed to have a good hand at surgery, I wondered why he would want to spend his career at this remote place and had my doubts.

After ten minutes, we started on the next case. This one was a lance naik who had three artillery shell splinter injuries on both legs. The left tibia – the shin bone – was fractured too, but I was not trained to set the fracture nor did I have the means to do it. There was nothing heroic to be done in this case. I just had to clean the area to prevent infection from spreading and remove the dead tissue and other debris. Then I identified and marked the tendons and nerves and attempted a partial closure of the skin. The final surgery to fix his leg would be done at an orthopaedic centre in the hospital to which he would be transported.

Suddenly, there was a terrible booming noise right in the room, and for a moment I was sure that the inevitable had happened – the hospital had been hit by an enemy artillery shell. This was the end and we would all die … but nothing happened. No sign of any fire nor any alarms or shouts. Major Ramprasad gave me a sheepish smile and said, 'Actually, this anaesthesia machine is quite old. It was the

A Proper Reception

pipes bursting. I knew this would happen, and that's why I had asked Delhi for a new machine a while ago. But there has been no response to my request.'

I looked towards where he was pointing. It was a vintage Boyle's machine, probably from the 1960s. The number of cases here were so few that it had never been upgraded. But now, with so many cases within a week, it couldn't cope. The bureaucratic tangles at Delhi meant that the pleas from here were just not heard.

The next case was a twenty-three-year-old sepoy with an avulsion and a dislocated bone at the right elbow. The blood vessel was visible, still pulsating, but unharmed. It required anaesthesia for about thirty minutes. Major Ramprasad decided to administer dissociative anaesthesia with a ketamine injection. It is a kind of anaesthesia in which the patient is not completely unconscious. He feels no pain, but may talk incoherently at times.

The surgery started after the patient was deep under anaesthesia. Once the necessary debridement was done, the patient started coming out of anaesthesia. He seemed to be from a village in Punjab, because he suddenly started shouting in Punjabi. He was only

The Kargil War Surgeon's Testimony

semi-conscious and still disoriented. 'Oh, you mother******, just wait till I get you,' he yelled. 'Shooting from behind the bunker, you dogs! And that bi***, who does she think she is! You bloody Benazir, just you wait!'

It was 2 a.m. and we were a bit tired, but the sepoy's shouts jolted us all wide awake. All of us were amused. In his reduced mental state, the poor fellow thought that Benazir Bhutto was still the prime minister of Pakistan. Despite that, he was still clear that he had to fight for his country, no matter what. It showed the spirit of the die-hard Indian Army soldier. They give their all for the country with no questions or doubts.

The other cases were brought in to the theatre one after the other. A sense of fatigue and drowsiness slowly set in, and my movements became mechanical. By the time I finished operating on all the casualties, it was 7 a.m. The cases were all stable, and I returned home from work when others were just starting their day. My first day of surgical experience at Kargil was over.

In my room, the hole in the roof allowed in bright sunlight. I knew that I could get only an hour or so of rest because I had to get back to the hospital to re-evaluate the casualties

A Proper Reception

and then arrange for them to be transported to Leh or Srinagar. I thought about my initial apprehension about getting no surgical experience in this posting because the hospital did not have a functional operation theatre. How the situation had changed!

I thought again about the cases from the night before. They were managed satisfactorily, although I did have the experienced Dr Kachu at hand. But what if some case goes wrong? What if I'm unable to handle a situation and someone dies by my hand? I reminded myself of the words from the Bhagavad Gita: *Karmanye vadhikaraste ma phaleshu kadachana* – keep performing your duties without worrying about the result.

From the open door of my room, I could hear strains of the gurbani being recited by the infantry unit in the gurdwara nearby. These mingled with the chimes of bells at the temple near the hospital. I could see the shining blue dome of the Kargil mosque across the river, from where a faint azaan reached my ears. The pious were praying for peace and everyone's well-being, while their fellow humans indulged in violence against each other. We are indeed a strange species created by nature, I thought.

8

Mind over Matter

I returned to the hospital at around 10 a.m. – a bit late but considered acceptable if there weren't any serious emergency situations. Those who had been operated upon had to be transferred out either by road or by helicopter. I had to list the total number of patients, assign the order of priority for each of them and recommend the type of transport required. The rest would be done by Captain Sugumar. But when I arrived, the discharge papers had already been completed by Major Anupama. She had left space for me to put my final notes.

'Why did you write the notes without me?' I asked her. 'What if something goes wrong? Suppose a patient's condition worsens and he cannot be transported?'

'Don't worry,' she replied. 'Nothing will go wrong. You've done a fine job.'

Mind over Matter

By 1 p.m., we had finished the work at hand and the ward was empty. It was time for lunch.

'What did you think of Dr Kachu?' Major Ramprasad asked me during the meal.

'He seems to be quite an experienced doctor,' I said, not sure what he was implying.

'Do not talk too casually to him,' said the major. 'Keep the conversation purely professional.'

'What do you mean?' I asked, intrigued.

'There had been no firing for a couple of days before the day the ammunition dump was hit,' he said. 'It was suspicious that all of a sudden the artillery shelling seemed to almost target the ammunition dump. Just before that happened, military intelligence sources had overheard a phone conversation. It was a woman's voice, someone from Kargil who was communicating with someone in Pakistan.'

I was shocked.

'As it happens, Dr Kachu Hussain's wife is the daughter of a retired Pakistani brigadier. There is strong suspicion that she may have been the person giving information to the Pakistani Army about the ammo dump. Strange, yes, but in war, all possibilities have to be considered. So we have received a directive that if required we can call Dr Kachu for help, but we are not to share any information with him. He may be completely innocent and perhaps unaware of any goings-on. But we have to be careful. You should know about this, so I am telling you.'

I wondered if it could be true. Dr Kachu seemed harmless. Could he be involved? Then I reminded myself that it was not my job to do the thinking. I had come here only to perform surgery. I decided to kept my mouth shut and not communicate much with Dr Kachu. I had managed a few hours of sleep after lunch when I was woken by some loud clangs and the shouting of men outside.

Stepping out, I saw a few soldiers digging a huge pit in front of my room. Some others were plastering the walls of the pit with stones, big rocks and cement. I understood that they were building a bunker to protect us from the enemy artillery shelling. We would probably have to stay there at night and during our periods of rest. Iron sheets and logs for the roof were scattered all around. The logs would be layered with the iron sheets, with sandbags in between. The rest of the structure would be below ground.

Mind over Matter

I noticed another small pit near the bunker. It was covered by a tin sheet. I thought it was a smaller bunker and tried to look inside by lifting the tin sheet. I was stopped by one of the soldiers just in time.

'Don't, sir!' he called out. 'Do not do that.'

I asked him why.

'Sir, that's the pit for soaking sewage. You wouldn't want to fall into it.'

At 7 p.m. we were informed that eight casualties would be arriving later that night. We had an early dinner and awaited the arrival of the patients. The drill started as soon as they arrived: a preliminary examination and basic documentation, triage, X-rays, resuscitation, detailed documentation and preparation for surgery. We found a similar pattern of splinter injuries in the arms, legs and chest. There were a couple of cases of bullet wounds as well. None of the cases were very serious.

The patients kept being wheeled into the operation theatre one after the other. We spoke little, restricting ourselves to: scrub, drape, pass the forceps, scissors, suck this area, ligatures, artery forceps, and hydrogen peroxide, saline and betadine dressing. After every surgery, we took a ten-to-fifteen-minute break, during

The Kargil War Surgeon's Testimony

which we wrote down the surgical notes and cleaned the theatre. Then the next patient was brought in, and we started again. This continued till 6 a.m. Dragging my feet, I returned to my room for some rest.

The same thing happened the next day when another nine casualties arrived in the evening.

'Why do they always come in the evening?' I asked one of the hospital staff. He told me that our soldiers were trying to move up the slopes to recapture the peaks. The slopes have steep gradients and are completely barren. So if they are struck by mortar shells or gunfire during the day, they have to lie there till the evening because the people who carry them down have to avoid getting shot at during daylight hours. After dark, the injured are carried back to the base slowly throughout the night, either on stretchers or in ambulances. Then they travel the whole of the next day to finally reach the hospital by the evening.

That evening, my body started aching after three surgeries. I felt feverish and my movements were a bit slow. Thankfully my mind was alert. By 3 a.m., I had finished five surgeries and was completely exhausted. The anaesthesiologist would get to sit on a stool and supervise when the surgery was being done, and the assistants worked in shifts. But I had to remain standing throughout. Yet, there was no question of stopping. I had to go on. More patients were waiting.

When I was in school, I had read about Roger Bannister, who was the first to run a mile under four minutes. In those days, it was considered impossible. In the last lap of the record-breaking run, his body was in severe pain. It was then that his mind took over. He surged ahead as his mind eclipsed the pain in his body until it became barely perceptible. He touched the finishing tape with a time of 3 minutes 59.4 seconds. I was obviously no Roger Bannister, but I drew inspiration from his story that day as my body ached and refused to work. My mind took over, my movements became mechanical and I could no longer feel the pain. I slowly finished all the surgeries.

The routine remained the same: a small period of rest in the daytime followed by operating on casualties through the night. The days rolled on and casualties kept pouring in from Kargil, Dras, Batalik and many other places that I had never heard of. On some days there were dozens of cases and on others, only

The Kargil War Surgeon's Testimony

a couple of patients. Since nearly all the cases needed to be operated on, I was getting to do a fair amount of surgery. I couldn't help but wonder when it would all stop.

9

Major Cases

By the last week of May 1999, we were in an unofficial warzone. Even though war had not been declared, the reality on the ground was different. The situation in the Kargil sector had worsened and the families of officers had all left by then. The artillery and mortar firings interspersed with gunfire continued unabated, and there was a sense of dread in the air. We were definitely at the receiving end of the fighting. Our casualties were rising by the day and another emergency surgical site was opened in the Dras sector to take on some of the surgical load temporarily.

The Indian Air Force had joined the fighting, targeting enemy bunkers and intruder camps. It was not an easy task as they would have had to spot their targets from a height of 3,000 metres at near supersonic speeds. Whenever we heard the sound of the fighter jets, we knew that an air attack was on.

One afternoon, the telephone rang. 'Sir, an officer is severely injured,' said the voice on the line. 'He will reach you shortly.'

'Name and unit?' I asked.

'Major Vikram Shekhavat of the Jat Regiment.'

I had heard that name recently. 'Wait a minute,' I said. 'Wasn't he declared dead on a private news channel?'

'He was wounded yesterday, sir, but he is very much alive!'

'Reporters!' I cried angrily. 'They cook up all kinds of stories just for a sensational news headline!'

When Major Vikram Shekhavat arrived, I examined him and found that he had a wound in the abdomen on the left side. As he breathed, his abdomen rose up and down slowly and a bit irregularly. The X-ray revealed a long, jagged splinter was inside him. He had to be operated on immediately. This could be serious.

Upon opening him, I found a river of blood inside. I managed to clear it with suctioning. His spleen was shattered. Among the remains of the pulverized organ was the splinter that had caused the injury. Apart from damaging the spleen, it had broken two ribs and damaged the diaphragm and the pleura – the covering of the lung. This was going to be a major surgery.

I removed the spleen after ligating the main vessels supplying blood to it. Then I cleaned the ribs and smoothened their edges before repairing the diaphragm. Finally, I inserted a tube for the lung to expand and recover. The surgery took three hours. As he was coming out of anaesthesia, the injured officer muttered, 'Doc, will I be able to fight again?'

'Of course you will,' said Major Ramprasad. 'But for now, take some rest.'

That was the first major surgery performed in Kargil, and as an independent surgeon, I felt satisfied. I was certain the patient would be all right. I had checked and rechecked everything to the best of my knowledge. Major Vikram Shekhavat was taken to Srinagar the next day by an air force helicopter. He was stable when boarding, and the hospital in Srinagar informed me later that he was out of danger.

The Kargil War Surgeon's Testimony

The same afternoon, a lance naik was brought in by a lieutenant colonel. He had a deep wound in the right side of his back and his abdomen was slightly swollen. The officer told us that they had been travelling by Jeep from Leh to Kargil, with the lance naik driving. After a while, the officer asked the driver to take a break and took the wheel himself. As they approached Kargil, an artillery shell exploded just behind them and a splinter pierced the passenger seat, hitting the lance naik from behind. It was strange luck. Had he not offered to trade places, it would have been him and not the lance naik lying wounded in the hospital.

During the surgery, I found that the splinter had just about missed the spinal cord, the bigger blood vessels of the abdomen and the right ureter. If any of those had been hit, the injury would have been fatal. The splinter had torn the small intestine at five places and had damaged the mesentery of the small intestine. (The mesentery is a flat, fat-laden, fan-shaped tissue commencing at the proximal intestine, holding the entire small intestine in a partially mobile manner. It has numerous blood vessels, all carrying digested fat and protein-laden substance to

Major Cases

the liver.) I cleaned the area and removed about twelve inches of the intestine before doing an anastomosis. Then I sealed the intestine with sutures. The operation lasted two hours and all seemed good. The next day, the patient was stable and was sent to Leh. I had successfully handled my first two major cases within a span of a few hours.

A few days later, a casualty arrived at about two in the afternoon. It was a twenty-two-year-old sepoy who had been hit by a splinter. About eight hours had passed since the injury, and he had gone into a state of shock. His pulse was feeble and his blood pressure very low. His abdomen was distended and the X-ray revealed that the splinter had entered his upper abdomen on the left side. The splinter seemed to be less than a centimetre long. Then why was he in such a terrible state, I wondered?

We commenced surgery immediately. On opening his abdomen, I found a pool of blood, approximately four litres of it. I panicked but kept operating. I had to cup out the blood with my hands as the suction was not enough. An emergency summons was issued for Dr Kachu. I could not locate the splinter but found that the stomach had been pierced. Was it inside the stomach? I checked and didn't find it there. I quickly fixed the damage to the stomach, but the blood kept filling up the cavity.

Finally, I found the splinter. It was lying between the stomach and the liver. Such a small splinter had torn his stomach and pancreas and lacerated two major blood vessels. The superior mesenteric vessels were damaged and the splinter was partly embedded in the liver. Dr Kachu arrived, but he too struggled to stop the bleeding. We washed the pancreas and removed unwanted debris while the patient kept bleeding.

Major Ramprasad kept his cool and arranged for fourteen bottles of blood from a nearby infantry unit. He slowly transfused it all into the patient along with an infusion of forty-five bottles of intravenous fluids. Dr Kachu and I struggled for seven hours. It was 11 p.m. when we finished the surgery. The bleeding had stopped but the patient's condition was critical. He had started developing complications from the surgery.

I hoped against hope that he would be all right. Major Ramprasad stayed back at the hospital, monitoring and resuscitating the patient. A nursing assistant kept pumping the oxygen bag kept under the patient's bed. On the walk back to my room, I prayed with a bowed head in front of the gurdwara. I was quite disheartened. The surgery had not gone well.

How did this patient have such a massive injury? I thought. And why did he have to come to me? What more could I have done? Dr Kachu said that we had done all we could. But I was not satisfied. I lay down in my room, unwilling to go down to the bunker to sleep. The world seemed a despondent place.

Sometime later, I was woken up by a terrible booming noise. The whole room shook and my bed rattled. It was around 1 a.m. I immediately knew that an artillery shell had landed very close to our living quarters. As I was wondering what to do, I heard a strange noise. It was a mixture of screeching and whistling that rapidly increased in intensity. It was the sound of an artillery shell travelling through the air at the speed of a bullet.

I was sure that death was approaching me fast. I could almost see it. Would this be my last day on earth? An eerie feeling came over me. After a fraction of a second, there was another noise louder than the first boom. My room shook again. But I survived because the shell had landed about fifty metres behind me. The lights went out and I was in complete darkness.

I stumbled out of my room with my sleeping bag. And then another shell landed somewhere in the vicinity. They were definitely targeting the hospital. I headed towards the bunker by pure instinct and jumped inside with my sleeping bag. I spent the rest of the night in the bunker. Though I was safe, my mind was not at rest. I kept tossing and turning, thinking about the patient.

The bad news was conveyed to me at 7 a.m. We had lost the patient overnight. A healthy and energetic young man was gone forever. Never will I forget the sight of his pale face and his distended abdomen. He had come to me for help – and what had I done? I was numb with guilt, shame and disgust. This was the first death that I had to deal with as a surgeon. Why me? I kept thinking. Why did I have to operate on him? I was not sure that I could ever forgive myself.

Major Cases

I could not have my breakfast. Major Ramprasad and Dr Kachu tried to console me, but to no avail. Later in the day, I called the hospital in Srinagar, where a professor of my postgraduate course was posted. He heard me out, listening to the details of the case silently and patiently. When I finished, there was a few seconds of silence. I held my breath, tense. Then he said, 'I don't think we could have done any better even here. You did your best, don't worry.' Even that did little to pacify me. The day passed in a blur.

10

A Feast of Bullets

I found the situation in Kargil quite depressing and did not know what the outcome would be. Would an all-out war break out? One day, Captain Sugumar told me that there were some outlandish rumours circulating among the jawans that the enemy would soon come down the slopes and capture this entire area. They were saying that we had better get ready to leave this area through the Zanskar valley or some other route.

'Of course, I gave them quite a mouthful,' added the quartermaster. 'They shut up after that.'

'Yes, you did well,' I said. 'We will not lose so easily. Our men are struggling so hard on the peaks, we have to believe in them. They will never give up.'

I believed this from the bottom of my heart. This was the Indian Army, after all. And they had been joined by the Indian Air Force as well.

A Feast of Bullets

On 26 May 1999, we heard that one of our MiGs had been shot down by a missile fired by the intruders. Apparently, two MiGs had been out on a mission when one developed a snag. The pilot, Flight Lieutenant P. Nachiketa, had to bail out. When the pilot of the other MiG, Squadron Leader Ajay Ahuja, tried to find Nachiketa, he was shot down. Meanwhile, Nachiketa was taken prisoner by the enemy. There was no news of Ahuja.

There were fewer surgeries around that time, and I took the opportunity to speak with some of the less serious casualties. They were of various ranks. I sat beside an injured havildar who had been here for a few weeks and asked him what exactly was going on out there. He looked around hesitantly and then lowered his eyes.

'Don't worry,' I said, trying to reassure him. 'I am not noting down your name. It's just for my own understanding of the situation.'

He sighed, then began to speak. 'Sir, when the first intruders were detected, it was early May,' he said. 'No one was sure of the exact number of people who had crossed over. Some said twenty; some said fifty. It was during that period of confusion that Captain Saurav Kalia was sent on a patrol to assess the situation. But contact with him was lost and he has been missing since then. We have no idea about his whereabouts.'

He told me that after more Indian soldiers started getting wounded and killed, the authorities realised that something was drastically wrong. They understood that the intruders had not come in the dozens – there were hundreds or maybe even thousands of them. They had occupied all the strategic heights and posts along a hundred-kilometre stretch and had crossed two or three kilometres into Indian territory.

When the news reached New Delhi, there was a panicked reaction and more battalions were sent over. Soldiers were rapidly deployed to the heights, at over 15,000 feet above sea level. However, most of them were not acclimatised to high altitudes and many did not even have proper snow protection such as boots and jackets. Others were given damaged boots – rats had eaten through them and left holes in them when they were in storage. There seemed to be no plans in place for replenishment of essentials such as food and communication equipment.

A Feast of Bullets

I asked him if the authorities and the division commander at Leh had passed on the intel on the terrain to Army Headquarters. He replied that they should know the area well, so he wasn't sure why they were facing the problems. So it appeared that the commanders were somewhat disconnected from the ground reality of the region. The soldiers and officers were ordered to carry out an unrealistic task. Were we caught off guard by the deceitful Pakistani ploy? Or was it just a knee-jerk reaction, with orders given without being thought through? Perhaps only a later enquiry would reveal the truth.

The Indian soldiers had been ordered to climb up barren mountain slopes at gradients of 60 to 70 degrees. There was not even a blade of grass on them for support or shelter. The plan was to set up a basecamp within three days. Accordingly, they carried rations for only those three days, with the expectation that reinforcements would soon arrive. But it turned out the terrain was far more challenging than what had been assumed through helicopter surveys of the area.

The difficulties faced while climbing uphill in the face of enemy fire could not be imagined or planned for from a sand model exercise or a map. The soldiers could only cover half the required distance even after seven days. Moreover, snow tents had not been issued to all because of the rushed processes. As the soldiers struggled to climb up, they became easy targets for the Pakistani intruders. That was why we had such heavy casualties.

I was sure that though much would be written about all of this in future, many facts would remain hidden. Explanations would be offered and accusations would be made in the months and years to come. The narrative would be built from one sided-facts and a dose of rhetoric, and would be turned into history. The tale of the soldier who died on the slopes would never be heard. One of the laws of humankind is that history, factual or otherwise, is always written by the survivor. And that is how it will remain.

Lying silently in one corner of the ward was a young captain who was recovering from frostbite. I approached him next and asked how he had managed to sustain himself on the rocky mountain slopes. He replied that it was quite difficult. 'We had carried some dry rations,' he explained. 'We were to

A Feast of Bullets

eat one chapatti in the day and one at night, and for snacks we had some dried nuts and sugar candies.'

However, after four days, their rations were exhausted, and there was no replenishment from a backup team. They had to resort to eating snow and ice to satisfy their hunger pangs. 'Of course, we had other things to eat too,' he said with an ironic smile.

'Such as?' I asked.

'We could feast on a steady stream of bullets, sir!' the captain said with a sardonic laugh.

I tried to imagine a situation in which one is without food and subject to endless gunfire. I had no reason to doubt his story. He had nothing to gain by making up stories.

'What happened when someone was hit?' I asked after a short silence.

'Casualties were everywhere,' said another voice suddenly. It was a naik speaking from the adjacent bed. 'But trying to go to the aid of your injured comrade was suicide. We were clearly visible to the enemy during the day, so we could only do that after nightfall. A friend of mine was hit by a bullet in his right wrist, and he also had a broken ankle which didn't allow him to move. The injuries were not life-threatening, but none of us could go to his aid in the daytime. He kept lying there and bled to death.'

'How did you pick up the injured in the dark?' I asked.

'We silently crawled towards the wounded and dragged them to a safe place, like behind a rock,' replied the naik. 'Still crawling, we somehow pulled or carried them down the hill, sometimes using our belts as a makeshift stretcher. And all this time we had to ensure that the enemy did not spot us.' The casualties were then carried to a place where a nursing assistant or perhaps a doctor was available or where an ambulance was present. Sometimes the journey would take two days or more. The naik said he had reached our hospital three days after being injured.

I looked at him in disbelief. I saluted all our soldiers earnestly. Then I asked the captain about the involvement of the air force. He replied that he didn't know. 'They carried out a few attacks on the peaks,' he said. 'Then suddenly they went silent. Maybe after the incident of the MiGs going down, the higher-ups changed the strategy. Support from the air force would have helped us a lot, but now we have to fight alone. We had been expecting them to engage the enemy but that did not happen.'

I realised that I had not heard the sound of any fighter jets for the last four days and wondered what the problem could be.

'Then how much time will it take for us to recapture the heights?' I asked.

All the patients in the ward reacted with surprise at my question. 'It is next to impossible, sir!' said one of the soldiers. 'How can you get to the enemy if you have to climb a steep slope to reach them while carrying a load of twenty kilos and with no cover or support! They will shoot as soon as they see us. We will die like flies.'

It was so strange to see an Indian soldier speak so negatively. They are tough cookies, acknowledged as among the best in the world. But were they let down by the headquarters' strategy? Why? What these soldiers said matched what I had seen and heard so far. I could not understand how they would win the battle. What would happen next?

I wondered for a moment if I should note down their names and use their testimony to resist this injustice. But that could land them in deep trouble. Since they had confided in me, I must protect their privacy. So I will not mention their names. What was important is what they had to say.

Many officers of different arms of the military used to dine at our mess as it was the closest to the helipad. I once had the opportunity to talk to a Military Intelligence officer there. I asked him if he had any updates on the whereabouts of Saurav Kalia. The officer looked around before answering in a hushed tone, 'I'm not exactly sure, but we think he is being kept at a secret location in the interiors of Pakistan. In fact, in a televised interview on a private Pakistani news channel, their prime minister admitted that they were holding six Indian soldiers as prisoners. That was sometime around the end of May, I think. But after that, all reporting on this matter by Pakistani media has stopped. Perhaps they were pressurised by their government to keep things hush-hush.'

'Why don't we do something?' I asked. 'We must take it up at an international level. It would be too late otherwise.'

'Of course,' he agreed. 'We must do something, and we have sent our reports. Now

A Feast of Bullets

it's up to the higher authorities to take up the matter. I don't understand why there has been no action yet.' With that, he excused himself, leaving me perturbed.

I kept wondering what the problem could be. After all, Saurav Kalia was an officer of the Indian Army, and his team was with him too. Maybe they were all still alive and could return. We were losing time. Was the country not responsible for their welfare? But who was I to ask such questions.

I switched on the television in the hope of hearing some news about Captain Saurav Kalia and his men. There was nothing. I could only pray that things would not become any worse.

11

Tasting Menu

One day, I had finished my surgeries quite early. Most of the patients had been evacuated, and there was no news of any casualties arriving in the evening. But then I received a call from the commanding officer.

His tone was sombre when he said, 'A coffin of a martyr has just arrived here by helicopter. I would like you to go to the helipad and inspect the mortal remains.'

'Me, sir?' I said, surprised. 'But I'm a surgeon. I'm supposed to stay at the hospital in case any casualty arrives. A medical officer could—'

'If I've called for you, there is a reason for it,' said the senior officer. 'You will understand why when you get there.'

'Right, sir. I am on my way.'

The shelling by the enemy had stopped by evening. An ambulance took me to the helipad. I had my torch, some medical examination tools and my rubber stamp. We drove without switching on the headlights, as the lights could draw enemy attention from the mountain ridges behind the helipad. The driver and I did not exchange a word. As we arrived at the helipad, I found myself very curious about the person I had been asked to inspect.

At the far end of the helipad were a couple of bunkers in front of which two sepoys stood at attention. I headed in that direction in the silence. As I entered the bunker, a musty smell assailed my nostrils. Inside, there was a coffin made of very thick plywood. It was covered by the Indian tricolour. The flag was removed by a morose-looking lance naik and then the coffin was slowly opened.

The body of an air force officer lay inside. He was in his uniform with his rank badges on his shoulders. His identity card was strapped around his neck and his nameplate was over the right side of his chest. It read 'Ajay Ahuja'. So this was Squadron Leader Ajay Ahuja, who had been missing since his MiG was shot down by a heat-seeking missile as he tried to save his colleague Flight Lieutenant Nachiketa.

Nachiketa had been captured alive by the enemy, and the news of his capture had been aired on a Pakistani news channel. That had led to international pressure on Pakistan to release the flight lieutenant, which they did after keeping him in captivity for a week. However, though Squadron Leader Ahuja had bailed out from his stricken aircraft, there had been no news of his capture. Nobody knew about his whereabouts until then, when his body had been returned by the enemy.

I matched Squadron Leader Ahuja's face with his identity card and confirmed his known identification marks. There were bullet marks on the right side of his neck and chest. His left knee had a big wound, with a probable fracture. Was it because of a parachute landing gone wrong on a mountainous terrain? Or was it inflicted later on? There were blunt injury marks on his face with dried clotted blood over his nose and bluish discolouration on his cheeks. These were definitely not from a rough landing. It was evident to me that Squadron Leader Ahuja had been punched by strong fists and tortured before being killed in cold blood. I ruled out suicide as that wouldn't explain the two bullet wounds that had been inflicted from a distance.

Squadron Leader Ajay Ahuja had become just another name on the long list of martyrs.

Tasting Menu

Another pension document readied and monetary benefits distributed, a funeral march and a visit by a local politician ... and there the obligations ended. Another file closed. The Indian Air Force had lost a brilliant fighter pilot, but only his family would really feel the loss. A mother would grieve for her son, a wife would lose her beloved and a child would grow up without a father.

How fortunate Flight Lieutenant Nachiketa was, I thought, that strong diplomatic pressure from the United Nations had ensured his release. His colleague had not been so lucky. His lot had been an untimely and unfortunate death, fighting like a hero and trying to save his comrade deep inside enemy territory. The Geneva Conventions to protect human rights had not been followed in his case. I closed the coffin lid, saluted him and walked out of the bunker.

An army marches on its bellies, as the old saying goes. In the days of old, when an army marched through a village or town, the residents would share with the soldiers whatever rations they could spare. In fact, sometimes villages would be attacked and plundered if they did not provide the army with adequate supplies. Thankfully, we did not have to resort to such barbarism at the field hospital, as we received our rations from a supply depot a few kilometres away.

The supply depot consisted of about twenty ground shelters put up on a flat stretch of land called the 'plateau'. During the day, a steady stream of Shaktimans moved towards the plateau like ants carrying food to their queen. They would ferry rations and essentials such as fuel from the base depots at Leh or Srinagar. The officer-in-charge of the plateau was a major, a stocky man in his late twenties from Tamil Nadu. He would often accompany the ration trucks to visit the hospital and have a cup of tea with us. His updates on the warfighting would add a bit of zing to our tea break on the days he visited. Sometimes he would show us how to make filter coffee, the speciality of his home state.

On one of his visits, the major said, 'You people are working day and night. Why don't you join me for dinner tomorrow? Maybe we can get some good quality rations and have a bit of Old Monk rum.' Then he added with a wink, 'And if we are lucky, we'll also get to taste our

The youthful river Suru

The town of Kargil as it looks in the 2020s

The mountainous peaks near the Line of Control (LOC) which Indian soldiers had to climb in order to capture the heights

A close view of the same peaks near LOC – barren and rugged

Kargil receiving shelling

Pieces of enemy artillery shells retrieved from Indian soldiers during surgery

The operation theatre staff

The ward staff

Bollywood celebrities Shabana A'mi, Javed Akhtar and Suneil Shetty with the author

Salman Khan and Raveena Tandon with the author

Tasting Menu

"special menu"!' I knew what he was referring to. The plateau was a flat, unprotected area directly in the line of enemy fire. As a result, it always received the most enemy artillery shelling in our area. The major was actually inviting us to get a taste of close shelling!

I gave him a dry smile and said, 'Oh, that would be very nice. Thank you so much for the invite. But we can never really say how many casualties we will receive; what if tomorrow turns out to be a busy day? Besides, we don't want to disturb your work—'

'Don't worry, sir,' cut in the major, having none of it. 'I'm sure that if no casualties arrive by sundown, no one will come overnight as vehicles are usually not operated after dark. So you can certainly join me.'

He seemed determined to give us a taste of the 'plateau life'. I thought about it the whole day. Surprisingly, there were no casualties even at sundown. We informed the commanding officer about our plans for the next couple of hours and nervously drove towards the plateau by the light of the moon. As mentioned earlier, the norm of night driving in this region was to drive without headlights in order not to provide an easy target to the enemy.

The Kargil War Surgeon's Testimony

'We can sit out in the open,' said our host, 'but stay close to the bunker and no lights please.' As we relaxed in our chairs around tables laden with delicious snacks, a small fan buzzed nearby as Kargil, despite being at an elevation of 9,000 feet, had relatively warm summer evenings. We sat there in the darkness under the moon and millions of stars as the Old Monk flowed freely. We munched on almonds, cashews and walnuts, our minds unwinding after days of hard work.

Occasionally, we would hear the dull thud of an artillery shell landing somewhere far away. We were unperturbed because the ambience was perfect. Our chatter filled the night air until we felt an odd silence take over. The major shifted uneasily in his chair. 'I don't like this,' he said. 'I have a feeling that—' Before he could finish, an enemy shell landed nearby and the ground shook.

'They've started,' yelled the major. 'Get ready for fireworks!' Within seconds there was a screeching noise as though the sky was being torn apart and then a shell landed only about fifty metres from us. There was a blinding light followed by a deafening boom that rattled everything around us. The ground trembled like in an earthquake.

Tasting Menu

We jumped into the bunker and huddled together, petrified and breathing heavily. The major appeared amused. 'Now you've finally tasted the actual menu,' he said with a laugh. 'Hope you guys liked it.' After some time, dinner was served in the bunker. The food was delicious, but we couldn't enjoy it.

'See, this is how I live,' said our host. 'Every night that I survive is a bonus. Moving this depot to another area would mean several logistical hassles in the midst of a conflict. So we just continue here and hope for the best.'

Once the shelling stopped, we headed back to our Jeep. As we left, I saluted him and said, 'It takes some nerve to live here. Jai Hind!'

On the drive back, we felt a new appreciation for our life at the hospital. It was better than the plateau life, no doubt.

The peak of the Kargil conflict came in June 1999. Food supply became erratic as the trucks bringing us rations were regularly hit by enemy fire. The quality of the meals at the mess deteriorated, and we had to subsist on canned potatoes and dal for days. Fresh fruits, vegetables and milk were absolutely out of the question – we had stopped expecting such things at mealtimes. However, the situation in the forward areas was even worse. Most of the troops had to survive on just two chapattis a day.

After several days, we got word that a supply of fresh chicken was on its way to our ration depot. There was huge excitement in the mess as we discussed how we would prepare the chicken. Excitedly, we decided to prepare murg masallam for dinner. The dish was simple to make and the ingredients easily available, yet it was delightfully tasty. The quartermaster took extra care in explaining the menu to the chef. Some of us went to the market to purchase a few spices for the dish. Everyone was looking forward to a big feast.

Luckily, we only had two casualties that evening and neither of them was too serious. We finished the surgeries by 8.30 p.m. and rushed to the mess. Everyone was in high spirits and soon the rum began to flow steadily. We sat at the dinner table and ignored all mess protocols, banging our plates with spoons in eager anticipation. The mess havildar entered, saluted and ushered in the mess waiters with the food. The chapattis were served before the lids were taken off the main serving bowls. A delicious aroma hit our nostrils as the steam rose up in the air.

A waiter started ladling the curry and serving it on our plates with a flourish. We looked at our plates and in a flash our delight disappeared. On our plates was a dish of cabbage. We stared at each other, speechless. Within moments, our astonishment gave way to extreme indignation.

'What on earth is this?' I thundered.

'Cabbage, sir,' replied the mess havildar. 'Cooked with masala.'

'Damn you! We can see that it's cabbage! Where's the chicken that was meant to be on the menu today?'

'They flew off, sir. Some died.'

'Are you trying to make fools of us? I'll order a court of enquiry and subject you to summary court martial. This is a war scenario. You'll be punished very severely, mind you! What kind of a joke is this?'

'Sir, believe me. It's not a joke. I had myself gone to the plateau to collect the rations. But an hour before we arrived, the plateau received enemy fire and one shell landed right on the shed where the chickens were being kept. The shed burst into flames and many of the birds were killed in the fire. The rest flew off. It was impossible to salvage the situation.'

The havildar looked very apologetic. We were aghast. What rotten luck. Of all the places, the chicken shed had to be a target, and that too today! 'Damn those Pakistanis,' I said. 'May they rot in hell. Let them go to jahannum!' Our despair turned into exasperation as we ate the masala cabbage while trying to imagine it as murg masallam. We cursed while eating.

When we came out of the mess in frustration after finishing our disappointing dinner, we heard the dull thuds of artillery fire in the distance. A war was on and our soldiers were trying to climb up treacherous mountains to fight the enemy. Perhaps they had not eaten a proper meal for days; they may even be surviving just on ice. Yet they continued to fight with all their might. And here we were complaining about our food just because it wasn't what we were expecting. I hung my head in shame as I realised this, and my frustration and exasperation faded away.

12

A Shocking Discovery

Though the fighting became more intense, the arrival of casualties at our hospital became relatively infrequent. That was because most casualties were now being evacuated to the new operation theatre that had been set up at Ghumri, near Dras. The fighting too had mostly shifted to that sector. By then, India had named its conflict response Operation Vijay, and it was now known to the wider world that the two South Asian neighbours were at war. Pakistan continued to deny it had ever sent any soldiers or militants across the Line of Control.

We heard that the foreign minister of Pakistan, Sartaj Aziz, was coming to India on 11 June to hold talks about the Kargil conflict. I hoped the two countries would find an amicable solution to bring an end to the war. The day before Aziz's visit, an army officer walked into the mess, confused and in shock. From his face, I could tell that he had been through some trauma. He staggered towards a chair and begged for some water, which was immediately brought for him.

'What is the matter?' I asked him.

'Sir,' he replied slowly, 'I've seen them.'

'Whom?'

'Captain Saurav Kalia and his men.'

'Oh, have they been found? How are they?'

Others gathered around too, wanting to know more.

'Their bodies were handed over to the post near Kaksar, sir.'

I was thunderstruck.

'Bodies? You mean ...'

'Yes, sir. And not ordinary deaths, sir. I have never seen such horribly mutilated bodies ... their nails had been pulled out, their earlobes cut away, their eardrums punctured, their eyes gouged out and their bones broken. Even their penises were cut off. The wounds were old, sir, indicating that these injuries were inflicted on them while they were alive. And then they were shot from close range. It was a terrible sight, sir. I had to examine their wounds and certify their deaths.'

A Shocking Discovery

No sooner had the officer finished speaking than he rushed towards the washroom. None of us could move. We were stunned, mute, frozen to the spot. How could this be? I thought. Could the Geneva Conventions be simply ignored like this? Besides, could any human being do such a thing to begin with?

I had feared that something like this would happen after seeing what they had done to Squadron Leader Ahuja. It had been three weeks since Captain Kalia had gone missing, but the Indian government seemed not to have escalated the matter to international authorities to prevent just such an eventuality. I was in the mess for lunch but had lost my appetite. I quietly returned to my room.

That evening, two casualties were brought in from Batalik. I operated on them silently, my mind still troubled. I kept thinking about the enemy's act of barbarism. It was cold-blooded murder with torture. Even the worst criminals are not tortured this way. These men were just soldiers. Why had India not raised an alarm? Had they failed to understand the gravity of the situation? I was convinced their act of omission was partly responsible for these soldiers' fates.

The Kargil War Surgeon's Testimony

When Flight Lieutenant Nachiketa was captured by the enemy, the air force headquarters had forcefully demanded that he be handed over immediately. Was a similar demand made in the case of Captain Saurav Kalia? The Military Intelligence officer I had spoken to was not aware of any such matter being raised nor could I find any news or media report confirming steps taken to secure his release.

The country became numb with shock as the news spread. The defence and external affairs ministries and human rights organisations released their usual official statements addressing the tragic event while the United Nations and the rest of the world watched. The talks with the Pakistani foreign minister led to nowhere. Perhaps that was what the Pakistan army intended all along, to commit an act that would make India lose its restraint and declare open war. Then the international community would come to Pakistan's aid and the Kashmir issue would be highlighted as per their ploy.

But the Indian government did not play along, and there was no declaration of war. The ongoing operations continued as before. But in a change of strategy, India increased diplomatic

A Shocking Discovery

pressure on Pakistan – including from an old Pakistani ally, the United States. The Bofors guns stepped up the offensive, and the Indian Air Force once again joined the fighting. Every soldier through the army ranks was seized by an intense anger after the initial shock. If any Indian soldier had been unsure of the outcome of the war before, he was now fiercely desperate to hand the enemy a thorough thrashing.

At the hospital, the wounded soldiers began hounding me, asking for permission to head back to the battlefield. 'We do not mind more deaths and casualties,' they would say. 'No matter what, we will reach the intruders and kill those dogs! They are not fit to be called humans. We will not spare even one of them!'

It was the second week of June, and I could feel that the tide had turned. The Indian soldier had come alive with passion. There was nothing that could stop him.

The Bofors guns started pounding away at the intruders' bunkers and at posts occupied by Pakistan in the Dras sector. The air force took their attack to Muntho Dhalo, a fortified camp deep in Pakistan territory. But no battle is won until the ground is captured, and that was the job of the infantry. With air support

The Kargil War Surgeon's Testimony

and backed by the heavy firepower, the Indian Army recaptured several peaks along the Line of Control.

With the fighting in full swing, casualties were on the rise. The number of surgeries at the hospital in the Dras sector increased until the operation theatre there was hit by enemy fire. Thankfully, no one was injured. The hospital was moved, and the new establishment took care of the casualties from that sector. Our hospital managed the casualties from the Batalik, Kargil and Kaksar sectors.

13

Meeting the Press

On occasion, we had to treat civilian casualties too. Our hospital was just across the river from the town of Kargil, which often received enemy shelling. The civilian casualties were not treated any differently from army personnel. When human lives were at stake, it did not matter whether they were part of the military or not. Once it was possible to move them, they were shifted to the hospital at Minji, where Dr Kachu Hussain worked.

One day, I received a call from Dr Kachu. He told me that a large number of casualties had come to his hospital and he required my assistance immediately. At first I was surprised that he was asking for my help. I was just a rookie surgeon ... did it mean he had confidence in my surgical skills? I felt flattered at the thought of such a senior surgeon asking for my help and rushed to the hospital at Minji after securing permission from the commanding officer.

Dr Kachu was in surgery. I was led to the operation theatre, where I scrubbed up and joined him. The surgery at hand involved a wound in the patient's chest. Suddenly, the doors of the operation theatre opened and half a dozen people entered with cameras and video equipment. The cameras started clicking and flashes started going off.

Dr Kachu did not seem to care about the whole thing. 'Oh, just some press photographers,' he muttered to me. But for me, it was a mega event. I got overexcited at the idea of being photographed and appearing in the papers! What a great feeling! It was my first time being photographed this way.

I had to keep my eyes on the surgery too, of course, but as soon as we were done with the operation, I sent my assistant to give the press my details. But it was too late – they had already left. I had missed the bus! It felt like losing the opportunity of a lifetime. I returned to Kargil with a heavy heart.

Meeting the Press

A few days later, the commanding officer called me to his office and asked for a summary of all the casualties I had performed surgeries on and the general modes of their treatment. I did as I was told but wondered why he was asking for this when it was mentioned daily in the morning sitrep.

'Sir, I hope I haven't committed a blunder?' I said carefully.

'Oh no, nothing like that,' responded the officer. 'There is going to be a press conference, and I have to say something about the casualties and how we are treating them.'

The idea of being near the press again got me excited. 'Sir, may I come with you just to watch the goings-on?' I asked.

'You? What will you do there? You are not required.' Perhaps my face showed my disappointment at being dismissed thus, for he changed his mind and said, 'Well, OK, if you want to come, then report here at four-thirty. We will go together.'

I reached his room a little before 4.30 p.m. There was a bustle of activity there. I saw his orderly polishing his shoes, while a sepoy placed a new combat cap near his neatly ironed uniform. The commanding officer

The Kargil War Surgeon's Testimony

was writing a summary of the management of war casualties at our hospital. 'Just in case I cannot recall all the details,' he said to me. Then he gargled with warm water and popped some cough lozenges into his mouth. With that, we were ready to proceed to the press conference.

The site for the conference was near the helipad. There was a big crowd of reporters being briefed by some senior officers. The commanding officer jumped out of the Jeep and headed to the action, followed by me. He walked up to a colonel to seek permission to begin the interview. 'I hope you have prepared yourself and you know what to say and what not to say,' said the colonel. The commanding officer replied in the affirmative.

Suddenly, to his surprise, the colonel said, 'Actually, I was thinking that we should let a junior officer speak at the press conference. That will make a better impression as they are the ones actually managing the show.' He looked around and spotted me. 'Hey, you there,' he called. 'Aren't you the surgeon at the Kargil field hospital? Can you speak at the press conference?'

'Me, sir?' I responded in surprise. 'Yes sir, I can …'

Meeting the Press

The commanding officer looked stunned at the turn of events. He must have been cursing himself for bringing me to the press conference and allowing me to steal his thunder. He stood rooted to his spot like a pillar of stone as I walked past him and headed to the press conference with the colonel.

On the way, the senior officer briefed me about what not to say. He was confident that I would do well as I was the surgeon who was dealing with the casualties hands-on. But I was worried about my appearance. I had no brand-new cap, my uniform was not ironed and my boots were unpolished. I told myself that there was nothing to fear. I would simply say that we had done everything to the best of our capabilities.

I reached the site where the conference was being held. There were about thirty reporters waiting for me. I recognised one of them. She had short hair and was dressed in jeans. It was none other than Barkha Dutt of Star News, who shot to fame during the Kargil conflict by bringing the war to the drawing rooms across India. The cameras focused their lenses on me, and a dozen microphones were set in front of the table where I was seated.

The Kargil War Surgeon's Testimony

The press conference started and I was hit by a barrage of questions from every direction. Three or four reporters shot questions all at the same time:

'How many casualties come here and from where?'

'What kind of surgeries are performed?'

'Are there injuries from the cold, such as frostbite?'

'What are the processes for evacuation?'

I answered all the questions steadily and the reporters scribbled my answers on their notepads. From the corner of my eye, I watched for any signals from the Intelligence Corps officer who was monitoring all my statements. After about fifteen minutes, it was time for the last question. I was asked, 'Would you treat a wounded enemy?' I replied that I hadn't handled any such casualty. 'But if I did,' I added, 'I would treat him the same way that I would treat an Indian soldier.' With that, the press conference ended.

The colonel appeared pleased with my answers. But I didn't have the heart to look at the commanding officer, who stood all alone in a corner looking dejected. I felt sorry for him, but what could I have done? Everything just

Meeting the Press

happened so suddenly. He did not utter a word during our journey back to the hospital.

There I found four casualties waiting for me. They had minor splinter injuries on their limbs. As I was examining them, a woman walked in with a video camera. She introduced herself as Richa Pant from NDTV and said that she was interested in taking some videos of the hospital ward and interview some of the patients. I was a bit uncertain about allowing her to do that, so I asked her to run her request by the commanding officer. The reporter left for his office. After a while, she returned with an official letter permitting her to film at the hospital.

The filming began. The commanding officer too dropped by a while later. After shooting a video of me examining the casualties, Richa Pant said, 'I would like to conduct an interview with the surgeon.'

'You may proceed,' said the commanding officer in a dry tone.

This time there were no handheld microphones. Instead, a small collar mic was attached to my shirt. After interviewing me for about five minutes, the journalist turned to the commanding officer. 'Sir, may I interview you, too?'

The Kargil War Surgeon's Testimony

I thanked my stars that the commanding officer was getting a chance to speak. During his interview, he occasionally glanced at the note that I had helped him prepare when giving his answers. The journalist left not long after that interview concluded. I was relieved that this reporter had salvaged what could have turned into a sour relationship between me and the commanding officer.

14

A Morale Boost

One evening, a call came for me from the helipad. A casualty would soon be arriving in a Cheetah helicopter. His condition was critical, and I was to examine him at the helipad and decide upon the next course of action. I set out for the helipad in an ambulance without delay. The sun was sinking behind the hills, and night was fast approaching.

Within a few minutes of arriving there, I heard the whirr of helicopter rotors. When it landed, I ducked my head to brace against the strong winds it had kicked up and ran to the helicopter along with a nursing assistant carrying an oxygen cylinder. Behind the pilot and co-pilot was a man in a dirty combat uniform. There was a big bandage around his head. He was conscious and attentive and seemed generally comfortable.

The Kargil War Surgeon's Testimony

Since I had to check how deep the injury was, I slowly removed the bandage. When it was off, I was shocked at the sight in front of me. There was an irregular hole about two inches in diameter in the front of his skull. Through that hole, his brain was visible. I could see that the frontal lobe of the brain was injured. But there was no bleeding, and his vital signs were normal.

I asked him if felt any discomfort.

'No, sir,' he replied. 'Just a little pain.'

I was stunned. I had never seen such a sight before. How could a patient with such a brain injury be talking coherently? This fellow had to go to a neuro centre immediately, or at the very least a hospital with an intensive care unit.

'Well?' Major Rajiv Dua, the pilot, asked me eagerly. 'What now? We have oxygen for him on the chopper if he needs it.'

'He will go to Leh right now,' I ordered. 'He will withstand the journey. Just fly at a low altitude.'

'Righto,' said Major Dua. 'Move back then.'

We stepped away from the helicopter and walked towards the edge of the helipad. Just before taking off, the pilot looked at me. I gave him the thumbs-up and he reciprocated. And

A Morale Boost

then all of a sudden, the enemy shelling started. One of the shells landed near the helipad. But there was no turning back now.

Even as the helicopter took off, another shell landed near us. But through that barrage of enemy fire, the Cheetah soared like a falcon into the sky. As I watched it fly away, I realised that my right hand had unconsciously lifted into a salute. It was a gesture expressing my deep admiration and respect for the indomitable Indian soldier and our daredevil pilots.

A few days after that a naik was brought to the hospital. He looked disoriented but was able to walk with some support. Though his vitals were normal, I noted that his face was extremely sunburnt. His skin was almost charcoal black in colour. Both his feet were of a similar colour and were covered with several small ulcers. He had been affected by frostbite.

I asked him if he didn't have snow boots and protective gear. The naik gave me a blank stare and mumbled something incoherent. I could not understand what had happened so I asked the people who had brought him there. They

The Kargil War Surgeon's Testimony

told me the story the naik had narrated to them before his mind started to wander.

The naik was part of a small group of soldiers moving uphill towards the enemy when they were fired upon. Some of his comrades were killed. The rest took cover wherever they could. The naik eventually lost his bearings entirely and could not locate any of his mates. The next morning, he found himself alone on the icy mountain ridges.

He wandered around alone for a few days, spending the nights in caves. There was nothing to eat, so he survived by eating ice. He had a weapon but no ammunition left, so he took cover whenever there was enemy firing. After about a week, he was spotted by another group of our soldiers and brought back.

I started to treat the naik by first working to fix his nutrient deficiency. However, his mental state showed no improvement. Intelligence Corps officers arrived to interview the patient to find out where he had been and how he had avoided being spotted by the enemy for so long. They were trying to find out whether he had been sent back as a mole by the enemy. During their questioning, they scolded him and issued loud threats, but the naik would just mumble

A Morale Boost

a few words and then go back to being silent. The Intelligence Corps officers finally gave up after four hours and walked out.

I wondered how I could cure him and decided to call the base hospital in Srinagar. One of my teachers heard the case and said, 'It seems to be a case of war psychosis. The death of his buddies and his own near-death experience – wandering around alone in plain sight of the enemy – has shaken him up. Send him to us. We will manage him.'

The patient was sent to Srinagar the next day.

Another patient I was treating had a bullet wound in his right shoulder, and he also said that he had fallen on some rocks. However, even after surgery, the man kept insisting that he felt giddy and could not swallow food. I wondered if it was because of a head injury. But five days had passed after his fall, and his vitals were all normal. There was something amiss.

Looking closely at him again, I noticed cracks at the corners of his lips. I told him to open his mouth and was shocked by what I found. His oral cavity was an angry red, with small ulcers all over the tongue, the insides of the cheeks and the back of the throat. He was suffering from acute vitamin-B deficiency. That was what was causing him difficulty in swallowing and leading to giddiness. I asked him if he had not eaten any fruits or vegetables for a while.

'I have just had three meals in the last three weeks,' he replied. I was left speechless. I couldn't understand how he was still alive, leave alone fighting on a battlefield.

The man was a sepoy of the Ladakh Scouts. He was a local boy, tough as nails. He probably would not even have gone to the hospital had he not been shot. He would have kept fighting until he fell and died out of sheer weakness and malnutrition. Fortune had saved him from that fate. I started him on double doses of vitamins and other nutrition. He was better in two days and was sent to Leh on the third day.

General V.P. Malik, the army chief, often visited Kargil. We would only hear about it on the day of his arrival. But somehow the enemy would always have prior information about the dates and times of his travels. During one such visit, as soon as the sound of the chief's helicopter neared, our location was pounded by enemy artillery

A Morale Boost

shells. Their target was the helipad, but due to the hospital's proximity to the target, it remained in danger of becoming collateral damage.

There were booming sounds and then a clattering like a hailstorm on the roofs of the mess and the hospital ward. It was caused by splinters from the exploding artillery shells. One of the splinters happened to hit a havildar who was standing on guard. He was rushed to us in a stable condition but with a wound on the right side of the back and a vague lump on the left side. The X-ray revealed that the lump was caused by a splinter that had become lodged in the chest. It meant that the splinter had entered from the right side of the back and, after fracturing two ribs, had travelled all the way to the other side of the body. It was stuck in the lungs, right behind the heart. Indian soldiers had to pay a price for the 'reception' organised for our chief by the Pakistani Army!

As we were examining him, an artillery shell landed barely fifty metres from us. There was a deafening noise and the ground shook. The patients who could run dashed for their lives and some of the others were carried to the bunkers. But I could not leave the patient I was examining and continued with my work. That was when

The Kargil War Surgeon's Testimony

one of the nursing assistants, Naik Ghesoo Singh Shekhawat, said to me, 'Sir, even if we get hit by a splinter, it doesn't matter – because you would be there to save us. But what will happen if you were to get hit? We will all be in trouble. You had better take shelter, sir.' While I did not quite like the idea of me getting hit by a shell, his words oddly made me feel quite important.

The surgery commenced. The entire route of the splinter through the body was checked for other injuries it may have caused, and then the splinter was removed. The damage to the lung and the fractured ribs was repaired, and a chest tube was inserted after the internal bleeding was stopped. The patient recovered well and was subsequently transferred to the base hospital in Srinagar.

Occasionally, senior doctors of the Army Medical Corps came to inspect the military medical setup at Kargil. There were some who expressed their satisfaction openly and there were others who simply nodded their heads after reviewing the number and nature of surgeries performed at our hospital. We once received a visit from Major General R.K. Jaitley, an

A Morale Boost

astute physician who had taught me at college. He examined all our records meticulously and spoke to several patients.

Among the major operations performed by me until then included splenectomy (repair of a damaged spleen); intestine resection and anastomosis (intestinal surgery); and thoracotomy (chest and lung surgeries). The major general commented, 'I tell the field hospitals at other locations all the time that if the team at Kargil can do such surgeries, then why can't you?' I looked at him in surprise. The statement was like a pat on my back. I wondered if his intent had only been to boost my morale. Even so, I definitely felt very happy that day.

15

Visitors

By the middle of June, we were receiving the occasional encouraging news about our troops capturing certain peaks and inflicting heavy casualties on the enemy. But the majority of the peaks were still with the intruders. The press came in large numbers to witness and experience the war and report on it. They came from all over India and even from abroad. Most of them were enthusiastic and inquisitive and all would ask interesting questions.

In India, the audio-visual media was slowly making inroads into the traditional domain of the print media. Some of the television reporters filmed our Bofors artillery guns firing in the high peaks and transmitted the footage to the drawing room of almost every Indian household. The reporters would come in dozens to our hospital to receive guided tours by an army liaison officer. It

Visitors

almost seemed as though they had come on a holiday.

They were especially impressed by Captain Mangla, a doctor at our hospital. They clicked photographs of her from different angles and published stories about this woman working and surviving in a highly dangerous environment. Major Anupama, the senior woman doctor at our hospital, chose to maintain a low profile and rarely appeared in front of the press.

The journalists also met the patients and spoke to many of them. After about an hour or so of interaction, the liaison officer would say something like, 'OK, ladies and gentlemen, it's getting late and we've got to cover Batalik too, remember? Let's go!' And with that they would board their waiting tour bus and leave.

Sometimes I felt like an animal in a zoo, put on display for curious visitors from the safe and comfortable world. Of course, our visitors praised and encouraged us and patiently listened to our stories. But were we the guardians of the nation helping ordinary citizens experience and understand the nature of war? Or were we like in a circus performing for their amusement? Either way, I soon became used to the press and gave interviews to the Press Trust of India, the

The Kargil War Surgeon's Testimony

Indian Express, *Hindustan Times* and the *Times of India*.

As I was walking back from the hospital one afternoon, I saw a dishevelled and disoriented person wandering around the mess.

'Are you looking for something?' I asked him.

'Um, yes,' he replied. 'I am actually looking for someone from the field hospital to interview for a story. Could you help me?'

I asked him to come along with me. On the way, I asked him if he was hungry. 'Would you like to have lunch?' I offered. His face lit up with relief, and I took him to our mess. After ordering lunch for the two us, I asked him his name.

He told me that he was Srinjoy Chowdhury from the *Statesman*. He had reached Kargil a few days ago to write a story for his newspaper. But when he had tried to check into one of the few hotels there, he was told that there was no vacancy. So he had spent his nights on the hotel portico and survived on instant noodles.

After lunch, I showed him around. As the authorities had become quite relaxed about the press, I was allowed to point out the artillery

Visitors

shells and describe the kinds of cases that we encountered at the hospital. He took down all the details, sometimes looking aghast. A few days after he left, a half-page report about the medical setup at Kargil appeared in the *Statesman*. Srinjoy Chowdhury had mentioned me by name. I took it as a token of appreciation for offering him lunch that day.

The number of visitors from the international press increased. Among them was the chief Southeast Asia correspondent for CNN. The man, an Australian, fell ill after a hectic tour of the Batalik and Dras regions and was admitted to our hospital. He was suffering from acute mountain sickness as he had rushed into his tour without adequate acclimatisation and rest. He felt better after a day's rest with some intravenous fluids and hydration. The next morning, he had aloo parathas for the first time, thanked me and left.

Then there was a reporter from Reuters who visited the hospital. He was an Indian settled in the United Kingdom. We became quite friendly. During our chats, he told me that there was a lot of difference between the Indian and Pakistani narratives about Kashmir and its problems. 'In India, politicians often have different perspectives on Kashmir, and the various political parties often disagree on the issue,' he said. 'That leads to confusion, and the picture is far from clear. Pakistan, on the other hand, always states the same thing every single time, and all political parties irrespective of their other differences maintain a consistent narrative on Kashmir. Most know, or feel, that it's a lie. But if a lie is repeated a thousand times, it becomes the truth, right? That is why the Pakistani narrative seems stronger than the Indian one.'

I was compelled to nod in agreement. He often asked to hear my stories about the types of cases I dealt with. When it was time for him to leave, he offered me a firm and warm handshake and said, 'Glad to shake that hand of yours, sir!'

Besides the press, there were some visitors who arrived with no idea about the dangers at their chosen destination. I remember an artist who had come from Delhi to capture the landscape of Kargil on canvas. Thankfully for him, he did not see or hear any artillery shelling during his

Visitors

stay. He might have made a mess of his painting otherwise. Or perhaps it would have been a masterpiece?

Apart from the army chief and other very senior officers, the VIPs who frequented Kargil and Dras were politicians. Defence Minister George Fernandes would often be in the area to have a chat with the soldiers to encourage them. Prime Minister Atal Bihari Vajpayee also visited a couple of times but did not have time to visit our hospital as there were far more important issues he had to attend to. As always, on the days of special visits, Kargil would receive extra artillery shelling from the enemy.

When I was a child, my mother used to tell me stories of her grandfather who had been in the Indian Civil Service. During the British era, it was mandatory for a bureaucrat to travel on horseback around the area under his administration to see the ground realities for himself. It allowed him to better understand the changes that the region needed. That explained their efficient administration of such a huge nation. If senior bureaucrats of the present day visited warzones for themselves to understand the challenges first-hand, would we fare better, I wondered? Perhaps the answer is yes.

16

Celebrities

After a hectic night of surgeries, we had shifted most of the patients to Leh, and the ward was relatively empty. Work was relaxed and I was sitting and chatting with a patient when he got up excitedly. 'Sir, look behind you!' he exclaimed. I turned to see a man standing at the door of the ward, seemingly unsure whether to come in or not. He was a good-looking man in a black T-shirt and jeans and with sunglasses on.

Suddenly, I thought I had seen him before. Where could I have met him? Perhaps he was a patient of mine ... or an old school friend? I couldn't recall how I knew him, so I asked, 'You were at Pune at the army hospital, weren't you? Or was it Delhi?'

The man looked confused and then said softly, 'Actually, my name is Suniel Shetty. I am from Bombay ...'

Celebrities

Of course! Suniel Shetty, the famous Bollywood actor! And to think I could not recognise him ... but I hadn't even dreamed of seeing such people in Kargil. 'Please do come in,' I said, trying to conceal my embarrassment. Suniel Shetty entered, followed by several other celebrities – including the lyricist Javed Akhtar and his wife, the actress Shabana Azmi. I also recognised Sharad Kapoor, who appeared on television but was not as well known. The film stars had landed in Kargil!

The purpose of their visit was to greet the wounded soldiers and boost their morale by talking to them for a while. They started enquiring about the patients, and I accompanied them into the ward. Shabana Azmi and Javed Akhtar seemed particularly interested in seeing the conditions of the patients and the conditions the soldiers had to live and work in.

The patients were very excited to see the movie stars. When they were asked about some events from the battle, they added a bit of spice to their narration. I knew that because they had told me about the same events a couple of days ago, but without the added flavour. Most soldiers expressed their desire to go back to the front and fight. Their spirit seemed to greatly impress the stars. I noticed Suniel Shetty even wiping tears from his eyes.

The news about the presence of the celebrities spread through the hospital, which led to the ward being overcrowded by people trying to get a glimpse of the stars. Staff who had never ever visited the ward – clerks, washermen and cooks, among others – were seen clicking away with their cameras.

Further pandemonium followed when another group of Bollywood stars entered the hospital through the office complex. The likes of Salman Khan, Javed Jaffrey, Vinod Khanna, Raveena Tandon and Pooja Batra walked in, accompanied by gleeful officers.

The ward was packed, with some of the patients with minor wounds joining in on the fun. The commanding officer suddenly called me over and pointed to one of the patients. 'Wasn't that fellow admitted three days ago with intense back pain and sciatica-like symptoms?' he asked. I looked closer and then confirmed that to be true. 'Then how is he jumping from one bed to another trying to get himself photographed?' bellowed the senior officer. 'Discharge him right away!'

Among the celebrities, I found Vinod Khanna, Javed Akhtar and Shabana Azmi to

Celebrities

be genuinely concerned about the wounded soldiers. The others were casual about the entire thing. Salman Khan kept cracking silly jokes throughout the visit. He wasn't even sure whether he was in Kargil or Dras or Leh. I don't think it made any difference to him at all. Raveena Tandon kept repeating the same statement to each patient: 'Hello bhaiya, how are you? Can you recognise me? I am Raveena.' When she said this to a semi-unconscious patient, the patient just closed his eyes. Javed Jaffrey tried to impress the hospital staff with his breakdance and Pooja Batra looked quite uninterested in the whole affair. She seemed keen to leave. I wondered if she was afraid of being in a warzone.

After about half an hour, the movie stars all left for the helipad to be flown to Leh. The euphoria remained even after they were gone. The soldiers moved around with their chests jutting out, as though they had just starred in a hit movie. Some people who had shaken hands with Salman Khan and Raveena Tandon said that they would not wash their hands for a couple of days. The autographs and other mementoes from the occasion were passed around and lovingly examined by all.

17

Shelters and Rations

As the conflict continued, India seemed to be gaining ground. Some more peaks had been captured by our troops, and international pressure had started building up on Pakistan. They were condemned around the globe for their unlawful intrusion past the Line of Control. The Pakistani intruders were now facing the heat of the Indian firepower. The memory of Saurav Kalia spurred the Indian soldiers on. With each peak they conquered, they gained a more commanding position to further the advance of their comrades, who would then move forward to capture the next peak.

At the time, Major General Mohinder Puri was in command of operations in the Dras sector. Apparently, before the events of Kargil, he had raised a concern regarding the remote possibility of a Pakistani attack over the Line of

Shelters and Rations

Control north of the Kargil sector. However, it had not been given too much importance as the idea was considered quite improbable. However, when his fears were proven true, Major General Puri was tasked to lead the Indian response, as military authorities were impressed that he had foreseen the problem.

Major General Puri was an astute leader who had a plan and knew his objective. He stepped up the offence with the Bofors artillery gun, which proved its efficiency and destroyed many an enemy bunker with direct hits from as far as twenty kilometres away. By thus eliminating the intruders, it enabled our soldiers to advance. The air force hit targets deep inside enemy territory, destroying bunkers near Dras and in Mushkoh Valley and Muntho Dhalo.

As the number of Indian casualties dropped, our workload lessened and we moved into a period of lull. The intelligence officer would often give us updates at the mess. 'We have captured quite a few bunkers and even taken some enemy soldiers prisoner,' he told us one day. 'Most of the intruders were regular Pakistani soldiers, with only a few of them being militants. Pakistan's stance that their army was not involved has proven to be completely untrue. For all practical purposes, it was an invasion and not an intrusion.'

He said that the enemy had planned the attack for almost a year. They had constructed fortified double-storeyed bunkers at least six months ago, before the onset of winter. The bunkers were well stocked with rations, weapons and ammunition. Some of them also had gas masks and lethal chemical weapons. If the enemy was planning to use them, it would go against the Geneva Conventions.

The officer added that the bunkers had proper telephone connectivity, and some of them were even equipped with Iridium satellite phones. The equipment used by the enemy was far superior to what the Indian soldiers were using. 'Basically, they had been well established at their locations for a while,' he concluded.

'That's terrible,' I said. 'We had trusted them all the while and followed the unwritten pact of winter-vacated posts.'

The intelligence officer spoke of several papers that had been recovered which revealed the kinds of incentives offered to the intruders, especially the foreign militants. Each of them was given a two-month contract that guaranteed a payment of about nine lakh rupees. It was

Shelters and Rations

about a hundred times an Indian soldier's salary of two months. Apart from that, they were also promised security for their families by the army.

'One of the many reasons why the intruders withdrew rapidly was that many of them received messages that the contract money had not yet been paid,' the officer said. 'The Pakistanis had apparently kept delaying the payment while insisting that they continue to attack the Indian soldiers. Some of the intruders were even told that returning back to Pakistan would mean death. That led to a sense of disillusionment among the militant intruders.'

The intelligence officer said that the Pakistani bunkers in the Dras sector contained rations, soap and tinned foods that belonged to the Indian canteen stores department. That was because the so-called Pakistani bunkers in that region were actually built by Indian soldiers for themselves before vacating for winter. They were stocked with these dry rations for future use. When the Pakistani soldiers occupied these bunkers, they obviously helped themselves to these supplies.

'There was another startling thing,' he said. 'In these areas, the military canteen is open to the local population as there are few shops in the local market. We suspect some of the supplies were bought by residents of Dras village and supplied to the intruders. Which means the intruders were eating Indian rations while they were fighting against India. But that's not all.'

I was intrigued and asked him to continue.

He told me that the Indian soldiers slowly discovered a peculiar situation in and around the villages of the Dras region: several villagers had deserted their homes and escaped to the Kashmir Valley. The army authorities broke into a couple of houses that belonged to local labourers and shepherds. Each of the houses had two rooms, of which one had the personal belongings of the owner – things such as utensils, a stove, clothes and some bedding. The other room was filled with huge sacks of rice, wheat and sugar and several tins of cooking oil.

When they investigated into why a poor labourer should have a stockpile of such rations, they found that those labourers had used up all their savings to buy supplies for the advancing intruders, who were expected to soon capture Dras sector. It was a well-conceived plan of treachery by the Pakistanis. Unfortunately for

Shelters and Rations

them, it had been ruined by the valour of the Indian soldiers.

I wondered why the locals would help the enemy. How would they benefit from doing so? Would a poor man choose religious allegiances over food? It had to be money. Their loyalty had been bought by Pakistani lucre.

But these discoveries did not matter to the soldiers fighting on the peaks. They were all focused on defeating the enemy. Without fearing death, they pressed onward. Snatching only a little rest by sleeping on the rocky slopes, they kept on climbing and charging ahead.

18

The Brave Indian Soldier

The steady stream of casualties had reduced to a trickle. Most that were brought in had suffered from accidents rather than from enemy fire. There were some instances of Shaktimans being hit by boulders or skidding off the mountainous roads. That stemmed from the increase in vehicular traffic movement in the region over the past month.

We received news that the advancing Indian soldiers had captured all of the Juber heights in the Batalik region. There was great rejoicing, and we threw a party in the mess with the extra rations that arrived from the plateau. In response to these setbacks, Pakistan increased the intensity of shelling towards Kargil, injuring or killing a few civilians.

Our Bofors guns returned the fire. They created havoc beyond the enemy lines as they could hit targets without any guidance from

The Brave Indian Soldier

observation posts nor any grid references. We often saw the red trail of an artillery shell fired from the Bofors lighting up the sky. It would sometimes fly right above our heads.

All the while, waves of press reporters kept visiting our hospital in search of stories. One day, we were visited by a group of foreign reporters, who watched on as I performed a bedside surgery on a soldier with a splinter injury in his chest. As I continued with the procedure, the journalists started taking photographs. That was when I noticed a man do a somersault over the bed of another patient to get to my side! He then started assisting me in the surgery.

I was astonished when I realised that he was the ward housekeeper! I guess he wanted to be in the photographs too and perhaps appear in a foreign publication. His regular job was the tedious task of keeping the ward clean of blood and discarded bandages, so I couldn't blame him for craving the limelight. I decided to allow him his stolen moment of fame.

At another time, I had to be in a video for the Aaj Tak news channel. By then the excitement I had felt during my first press interview had become a distant dream and I was sick and tired of the press. I did not even bother to ask when the interview would be telecast. I also appeared in a documentary film about the Kargil conflict. That was a bigger production, with special lights installed in the ward and huge professional video cameras involved.

I was told that the film would be on print in the archives for at least a hundred years. I found that remarkable. Would anyone even remember this war after a hundred years? Would these soldiers be remembered? It brought to mind a poem by Rabindranath Tagore that addresses the reader who might be reading it a hundred years from the day he wrote it.

Though it seemed as though we were winning the war, there was still a long way to go before we could be certain. Thanks to the television and print media, the people of India were united in supporting the war effort. Hundreds of postcards and letters from children from around the country started arriving. Some had poetry expressing pride, while others condemned the enemy. Various organisations sent sweets and snacks for the soldiers. No one knew a specific address to reach us. But if they wrote 'The Brave Indian Soldier, Kargil, Kashmir, India' on the envelope or parcel, the

The Brave Indian Soldier

post offices around the country ensured that it reached us.

Then blood donated by various people started arriving in packets at the field hospital. We did not know what to do with them. Though it was suggested that I use the donated blood to treat casualties, I felt that it was best distributed to the various non-military hospitals in Kargil and Dras so that the civilians of this war-torn region could also benefit from the aid we were receiving.

By the first week of July, the war was definitely headed to a result in our favour. Most of the peaks around the Dras region had been captured by Indian troops. Heavy casualties occurred on both sides as the intruders tried to recapture the peaks. On 4 July, we received news that the key peak of Tiger Hill had been secured by the Indian soldiers. There were celebrations in the air once again, and the Old Monk was brought out to accompany some mutton kababs.

The roads were now reasonably safe and good-quality rations were arriving in adequate quantities. As we filled our bellies, we saw the flash from the Bofors gun being fired and then heard a dull thud as the shell hit its target far away. It immediately brought to our mind the soldiers who had crawled up a peak among those barren mountains and were perhaps eating nothing more than some dry chapattis and groundnuts for a meal. And here we were rejoicing their efforts by gorging on good food and drinks.

The next day, I happened to be watching the television when an interview with an army officer was broadcast. He was tall with a beard and sharp features and came across as a dynamic young man. The officer was introduced as Captain Vikram Batra, who had had a lot of success battling militants at Sopore in Kashmir. After moving to Kargil, he had launched a ferocious surprise attack on a peak called Point 5140. After single-handedly killing three enemy soldiers, he had destroyed their post and bunker with a grenade.

'The Pakistanis are finished,' he declared during the interview. 'We will not spare a single enemy fighter.' But then he added with a twinkle in his eye, '*Yeh dil maange more* [This heart desires more],' echoing the popular Pepsi slogan of that time. He had declared his desire for more action, leaving those watching the interview very impressed with his enthusiasm.

The Brave Indian Soldier

With such leaders in the Indian Army, I thought, there was no doubt that victory was going to be ours. It was just a matter of time before they triumphed.

The following morning, Major Anupama came rushing to me and said, 'Come quickly and watch the news.' There was a broadcast of a report on the previous night's attack on the peak named Point 4875. Through the mist and fog, Captain Vikram Batra had led his men to the summit. At around midnight they had led the final assault on the enemy. After a brutal hand-to-hand battle, Point 4875 had been captured by the Indian Army. However, Captain Batra had been martyred in the attack.

Eyewitness accounts said that he had rushed into the enemy bunker himself, pushing aside a subedar who was attempting the raid. 'You have kids,' Captain had said. 'Let me do this.' Though he had shot the enemy soldiers inside, he too was fatally wounded. I stood in silence upon hearing the news. What a terrible loss for the country, I thought.

19

Enemy Soldiers

I heard tales of the Indian Army's advance from various sources who visited our hospital or the mess. The enemy was now retreating as the Indian soldiers recaptured one post after the other. We received a report about soldiers falling ill after entering enemy bunkers that they had captured from the Pakistanis in the Dras sector. They were displaying symptoms such as nausea, vomiting and swollen, red eyes and reported that there had been a weird smell in those bunkers. It was later discovered that the enemies had planted toxic chemicals inside the bunkers.

In other places, soldiers found it difficult to enter whatever remained of the enemy bunkers because of the stench emanating from inside. The enemy soldiers had been killed in large numbers, and their bodies had been abandoned by their fleeing comrades. They now lay there rotting, emitting an unbearable smell.

Enemy Soldiers

While Pakistan still held certain regions – such as pockets in Mushkoh Valley and the Shranguthi peak in the Turtuk region – political and international pressure was building up against them. It eventually forced Prime Minister Nawaz Sharif to reluctantly order his troops to retreat to their side of the Line of Control. That decision led to him being severely criticised by the citizens and armed forces of his country. Sharif appealed for an intervention from their old ally, the United States.

However, Indian diplomats had by then presented war files and reports with documentary evidence of Pakistan's misdeeds to the United Nations and various countries around the world, including the United States, and American President Bill Clinton dismissed Pakistan's pleadings. The Pakistani Army had initially refused to pull back behind the Line of Control but was now ordered to back off without delay.

Meanwhile, the press was invited to visit the Batalik region. Accompanied by senior army officers, they were taken to witness a special operation led by the Indian government. The mountainous warzone near Batalik was littered with bodies of Pakistani soldiers killed in action. They had been abandoned by their army because their nation had insisted on maintaining that their army personnel had not been involved in the incursions. Some of these bodies were lying in gorges or crevasses that were very difficult to reach. Our government launched the special operation to send trained Indian Army personnel to retrieve the bodies of the Pakistani soldiers.

As the press observed, the Indian Army soldiers descended hundreds of feet into the gorges using ropes and then raised the bodies to level ground in a risky operation. The bodies of the Pakistani soldiers were draped in their national flag and were given an honourable burial with a maulvi in attendance and all religious customs observed. The press reported on the events and the whole world took notice of it.

However, not everyone understood the government's intentions. At our hospital, some of the staff were quite indignant about it. 'Were they not the same breed of people who had tortured and killed Saurav Kalia and the others?' was the common refrain. 'Why, then, are we so sympathetic towards them?' I could understand the fury felt by many in our country. After all, our men had been mercilessly slaughtered by

Enemy Soldiers

these very same Pakistani soldiers. For a while, I too thought the same way.

Then I gave it some consideration. Were we to stoop to the level of the enemy and abandon the basic ethics of the armed forces? Should we not have followed the elementary principles of humanity and accorded respect to a fallen soldier, even if he was from the enemy? After all, he had only been fulfilling his duty. My deliberation led me to overcome my initial disapproval of our government's actions.

The Government of India had indeed done the right thing by honouring the enemy soldiers and giving them a respectable burial. We had shown the world that our country follows the Geneva Conventions and, more importantly, that we grant basic human dignity to each individual, no matter their allegiances and beliefs.

20

The Special Casualty

We moved into a long period of lull. The shelling had all but stopped and incoming casualties had greatly reduced. The feeling was that the war would end soon. One day, I was informed by Military Intelligence that a casualty was on the way and I was to immediately notify them once he had arrived. No further details were offered, which left me curious about the identity of this casualty. What was the need for special instructions in advance for what should be a routine affair? Was it a very senior figure in our military?

The casualty was carried in on a stretcher accompanied by two armed jawans. He appeared thin and weak. I observed injuries on his right leg and on the right side of his jaw. Only when his particulars were recorded did I understand – the patient was from the enemy

The Special Casualty

side. He was a sepoy in the Pakistani Army and had eleven years of service. He was the first prisoner of war brought to our hospital during this conflict.

I notified the intelligence officers as instructed. The man had been shot in the knee and face and required surgery. The intelligence officers arrived before the surgery could commence and asked if the patient was in a fit state to answer some questions. I replied that apart from being dehydrated, he was medically fit for questioning and gave them permission to proceed.

For about three hours, they asked him various types of questions: to establish how much he knew about us; to know more about the situation beyond the enemy lines; and to ascertain whether he had been planted as a spy. I was not allowed to attend the questioning, but their loud voices reached me clearly, so I know what was asked. The patient replied in a quiet voice, and there were no indications of any physical torture being used. In fact, the entire thing was recorded on video.

When the intelligence officers finally came out of the room, they appeared disgusted. 'Either he is too smart or he is too dumb,' they told me before walking off. From the look of the patient, I personally felt it was the latter. Regardless of his intelligence levels, he had to be operated upon, and I began preparations for that.

Before the surgery began, I chatted with the man to make him feel comfortable. That was when he surprised me by saying that he was a carpenter. 'There was a lack of regular infantry soldiers,' he revealed. 'We received orders that every able-bodied man in the area must proceed to the frontline. Along with me, barbers, cooks and washermen were forcibly sent to man security posts.'

He said the Indian soldiers attacked from every side and he soon ran out of rations. Their bunker was destroyed by artillery firing. During the follow-up attack, his comrades were killed and he was shot in the leg and the jaw. He lay there injured, but even after the Indian soldiers had left the area, he was not evacuated by anyone from his side. 'Every day someone told me that they would take me down to the camp the next day,' he said, 'but nobody did. Instead, we were asked to hold our posts. After three days, the Indians attacked us again. By then, we had run out of ammunition. As the Indians came closer, my companions left me in that injured state and fled into the darkness.' Eventually, the Indians reached his bunker, found him and carried him down the mountains. That was how he had ended up there.

I asked him what he thought of the medical care he was receiving from his supposed enemy. 'It's very good, sir,' he said, sounding relieved. 'I think it's better than what we have back in Rawalpindi.'

'How long has it been since you received your injuries?' I asked him.

'About ten days,' he said. And then suddenly he started sobbing. 'Sir, you are so nice. You are doing so much for me. I have children and a wife to look after. I hope I will be allowed to go back to Pakistan.'

'If you are allowed to return, what will you do once you reach home?'

'I will quit the army, sir. I do not want to fight any more. I will perhaps take up farming.'

Here was a man who was our sworn enemy, and yet he was praising the Indian soldiers and medical corps. Was he saying all this out of fear so that we would not harm him? Or did he genuinely mean what he said?

The Kargil War Surgeon's Testimony

I couldn't be sure, but I was certain of one thing: he was badly shaken up by the war. The fear in his eyes was real.

I got him to sign a consent form, and then he was wheeled off to surgery. Perhaps the sight of the operation theatre frightened him further. People with masks and caps stood around him as he was led towards a huge machine with pipes and tubes emerging from it. Perhaps he was wondering if he was going to be tortured now and if he would ever get to see his wife and children again.

'Sir, what are you going to do?' he asked hesitantly in a terrified voice.

'Don't worry, we will make you healthy.'

He moaned helplessly, unable to shake off his suspicions. He pleaded again to be spared and allowed to return home even as Major Ramprasad administered the anaesthesia.

I noted that his right tibia was badly fractured, and over the ten days since the injury, his wound had become gangrenous. The leg was just about held together by a piece of skin. The situation demanded an immediate amputation. That would have been the easiest way. But then I wondered if I would be accused of cutting off his leg because he was a Pakistani. Though the argument for proceeding with the amputation was quite strong in medical terms, I felt that a controversy would definitely ensue. I examined the wounded area again.

The distal part of the leg appeared pale, but the tissues were not dead yet. Maybe there was still some blood supply to it. I decided to carefully scrape off all the gangrenous bone and clean the area without damaging the remaining blood vessels. That might give a chance for the leg to survive. I did not perform the amputation. If the leg did not survive, then it could be revisited by someone else for further diagnosis. It took over an hour to remove a significant part of his tibial tuberosity. Another hour later, the wounds in the leg and on the face looked much better. I had done my bit, and it remained to be seen how he recovered.

The patient was moved back to the ward after the anaesthesia had worn off. The commanding officer ordered for him to be taken to a small cubicle beside the ward. That cubicle was reserved for officers. I felt that he could have stayed in the ward with some extra security. Instead, the cubicle received a new carpet and curtains and even a vase with flowers. Two extra guards were placed outside the cubicle even though there was no question of him running away in his condition. I wondered what all the fuss was about.

The next day, I understood the reasons for all the extra activity when military attachés from thirty-five countries arrived in Kargil to see the prisoner of war. They each talked to him through interpreters, and then he was interviewed by the press. This was part of the process to determine whether the Indian Army was treating the prisoner in accordance with the Geneva Conventions. After about an hour or so, the visitors expressed satisfaction about the care and medical attention accorded to the prisoner of war by the Government of India.

The next day, the patient left for Srinagar in a special helicopter. I thought that he looked healthier. As he was being taken away, I gave him a long look but he did not turn in my direction. Perhaps he felt that he was now a very important person, well-guarded, cared for and talked about.

I was later informed that his leg had survived at least for the rest of his time in India. He was repatriated on Pakistan's independence day, 14 August. I don't know how his subsequent

The Special Casualty

recovery went. But from his tale I learned a lot about the reality of the Pakistani Army. They were low in morale, ammunitions and even able bodies to serve as soldiers. We already knew that their diplomatic efforts and logistics were in tatters. Now victory for India felt like a formality. It was just a matter of time.

21

Pakistan's Treachery

As Indian soldiers reclaimed peak after peak, Pakistan knew the game was over. They made the prudent decision of asking the United Nations to broach a ceasefire agreement with India. They promised that their soldiers would vacate the warzone completely if a safe passage of exit was guaranteed to them. In any case, most of the warzone had already been taken over by the Indian soldiers by then. The Indian government accepted Pakistan's request, perhaps under international diplomatic pressure.

Safe passage for return was granted to the intruders for a three-day window, during which no Indian soldier could fire on or injure any Pakistani returning from their bunkers to Pakistan-occupied Kashmir. I wondered if it was a wise decision to come to that agreement. After all, we were all set for victory when

Pakistan's Treachery

suddenly our army's hands were tied. Pakistan has been known to backstab us in every war in the past. Were we falling into their trap again?

The Indians did not fire a single round of artillery for three days. The Kargil valley was silent apart from the sound of the Suru roaring past, and we could hear the chirping of birds after a long time. In fact, many of us were tossing and turning in bed, unable to sleep without the noise of the artillery fire in the background!

Even as Pakistan pulled out, it kept stabbing India in the back. Mines were placed all over Indian territory and by their bunkers at the Line of Control. Then our neighbours replaced all their demoralised troops and depleted supplies with fresh soldiers and ammunition. Their rations were restocked, and they prepared for another assault. On the other hand, the Indian soldiers lost their motivation and became disillusioned. They had been fully charged to take on the enemy but lost steam during the three days of ceasefire.

After the ceasefire ended, the Pakistanis changed colours like a chameleon, and the quiet of the valley was again shattered by their artillery shells, which resumed pounding

The Kargil War Surgeon's Testimony

Kargil and Dras. The Indian Bofors guns again returned fire and the Indian soldiers resumed their advance to the abandoned bunkers and the heights along the Line of Control. However, Pakistan's treachery bore fruit. The Indian soldiers now started getting injured and killed by the mines that the Pakistanis had carefully planted. Many soldiers lost their limbs.

The pattern of casualties arriving at the Kargil Field Ambulance were now very different. There were fewer cases of bullet or splinter injuries and more of severely damaged limbs. We tried to preserve whatever parts we could but most were damaged beyond repair. Amputations became common. We had again trusted, an enemy that was never to be trusted and the war had again reared its head. The days of bloodshed were back.

Our hospital received a visit from the distinguished dancer and choreographer Sonal Mansingh. However, there was hardly any excitement around as by then we had got used to visits from celebrities. Ms Mansingh came to the ward to greet all the wounded soldiers, entertaining them by reciting some patriotic poems written by Prime Minister Atal Bihari Vajpayee. She then sang a couple of songs and finally brought out her strong suit – dancing. She danced to 'Vande Mataram' and sang along. As she neared the end of her performance, we saw tears in her eyes.

Her voice choked with emotion, she asked me for a recording of her performance. 'I've performed at so many places but never felt this sort of an atmosphere,' she said. 'It truly gave me goosebumps. May you all be blessed and carry on your good work.' I did not think I would see her again and have the opportunity to give her a copy of the video recording I had made. Maybe someday I will.

On another day, two taxis arrived carrying some officers of the State Bank of India. They were accompanied by their wives. They had travelled through enemy shelling to reach Kargil simply to meet and talk to the wounded soldiers and congratulate the Army Medical Corps for their service to the nation. All of us were touched by their gesture. It was clearly not a publicity gimmick. There was no press or photographers accompanying them. It was a personal gesture of sincere patriotism. The interest and concern in their faces was apparent to all as they patiently spoke to each soldier and then handed him a Sony Walkman. Then they left as quietly as they had come. It was a heartfelt gesture not from celebrities but from common Indian citizens.

Soon after their departure, we received notice that the MLA of Kargil wanted to visit the field hospital. He belonged to the Congress party, which was not in power at the Centre then. He had received orders from the party headquarters in New Delhi to pay our hospital a visit. Apparently, deep concern had been expressed from the party headquarters about our situation.

Before long, the MLA and his entourage arrived and press photographers descended upon the hospital. The patients were dressed neatly and made to sit up on their beds when the MLA entered the ward. He was followed by local politicians carrying bags laden with slippers and pyjamas for the patients. Photographs were clicked and the whole episode was documented as a grand philanthropic gesture. The Congress party workers tried their best to stir the sentiments of the soldiers by telling them things like, 'We are with you!' However, the wounded soldiers were unmoved. They had seen enough of such melodrama.

Our next celebrity visitor made a better impression. She was none other than Bachendri Pal, the first Indian woman to have summited Mount Everest. Her team — most of whom were women — had travelled on motorcycles from Jammu to Srinagar and then onward to Dras and Kargil. They were on their way to Leh, from where they would go to Lahaul, the Spiti valley, Manali and finally Pathankot. They visited the ward and distributed sweets to the soldiers and heard their stories.

There were the standard smiles and photographs, accolades and patriotic spirit on display. And then Ms Pal said, 'I might have climbed Mount Everest, but I can definitely say that I could not have achieved the feat that you have — climbing the mountains with heavy loads while fighting against the enemy. We are all very proud of you, my brothers.' These words finally brought a smile to the faces of the soldiers. They were moved by the sincere praise from the woman known as the 'Daughter of the Himalayas'.

22

Hard Choices

The casualties eventually started decreasing again, but they still kept coming. On occasion, we received a large number of casualties all at once. One day, eight casualties were brought in together. Most of them had injuries of the lower limbs, probably inflicted by mines. But one had a splinter in his right elbow. Examination revealed no pulse at the right wrist. The radial artery pulse was not palpable. I wondered if the splinter was obstructing the artery at the elbow. Something told me that it could be serious, so I called for Dr Kachu before I started the surgery. He promptly arrived and joined me in the operation theatre.

We explored the patient's elbow and lower arm after removing the splinter. By then the patient's right hand was cold and showing a bluish tinge. It was evident that pre-gangrene was setting in. Then we discovered the damage caused by the splinter. It had shattered the right brachial artery, the main artery of the arm. That is why there was no radial pulse – there was no blood supply to the right forearm and hand. Luckily for the patient, the artery had gone into a complete spasm after sustaining damage and stopped itself from bleeding rapidly. Arteries are known to sometimes go into a spasm to prevent death from bleeding.

I had two choices before me. The easier option was to identify the two ends of the torn artery and seal them. The bleeding would then stop but the chances of survival of the forearm and hand could not be guaranteed. That would depend on the blood flow from the smaller arterial branches that move around the elbow. The other choice was a bit difficult, especially given the kind of hospital we were in. It involved mobilisation of the two ends of the artery and tying them together with a very fine suture. The procedure was called anastomosis and was usually done by specialist vascular surgeons with modern equipment and lighting in highly specialised centres.

I looked at Dr Kachu. He shrugged. Perhaps he had not done this kind of a surgery here.

The Kargil War Surgeon's Testimony

Then I remembered what Gabbar had said in the film *Sholay*: 'Fear is death.' I decided to give it a try. After all, what was the worst that could happen? If the anastomosis was unsuccessful, the hand would be as it already was. But if the surgery was successful, the hand could be saved.

We had no vascular instruments, so I brought out the clamps designed for holding intestines and covered them with wet cotton gauze. The artery ends were mobilised and loosened before being held very lightly by the clamps. I took off my glasses to adjust my vision for the close surgery. With a slow, controlled breath, I started the repair. The fine suture was hardly visible as I passed it round and round through the cut edges of both ends of the artery. Despite being quite nervous himself, Dr Kachu kept guiding me until I completed the anastomosis.

With bated breath, I slowly released the intestine clamps. Dr Kachu observed closely as the artery swelled up. A minuscule trickle of blood escaped ... and then there was none. The repaired artery started pulsating ... feebly at first and then gradually to a full, bounding pulse. The hand started turning pink. Major Ramprasad informed me that the pulse of the

Hard Choices

wrist could be felt. It was very feeble, yes, but it was there. The hand could be saved.

I was ecstatic. Dr Kachu was numb at first. Then as realisation of what we had achieved sunk in, he took off his gloves, lifted his hands and broke into a dance. We stared in amazement at the elderly surgeon dancing in the operation theatre until Major Ramprasad reminded us that the danger had not yet passed. We had to watch for reperfusion syndrome, in which the accumulated toxins of the pre-gangrenous element in the hand circulate through the whole body.

Major Ramprasad began the necessary treatment with intravenous fluids, antibiotics and many other drugs. The next day the patient was stable enough to be evacuated to Srinagar. That evening, I received a call from Colonel K.M. Rai, the vascular surgeon at the Srinagar base hospital. He too had been one of my professors at medical school. 'I have just received your case,' he said. I asked in a quiet voice, 'Is the artery still palpable, sir?' There was a brief period of silence during which my unease grew. It seemed like many hours passed before he said, 'Yes, it is. You did very well.'

Relieved, I asked if he was going to do any further surgery on him. He replied in the negative. 'What you have done is enough,' he said. 'His hand will survive. I'm quite proud of you.'

I thanked him and put the receiver down. It sunk in slowly. We had done it. That was the best surgery that I had performed so far. Me, a novice surgeon with just a few weeks of experience when I had arrived here. Who was I now?

The shelling had abated again and traffic had increased on the highway. We appeared to be close to victory. We were told all that was left was for it to be officially declared. During this period, a batch of six casualties arrived one evening. Their Shaktiman had skidded and toppled over, resulting in the deaths of two on board. The rest had been brought here. Two of them were in a critical condition, while the others had moderate injuries.

Of the two serious cases, one had a fractured rib and a swollen abdomen. It seemed to be an injury to the liver. The other person had a fracture of the right femur, with a swollen thigh. I decided that the first casualty was more serious and had to be dealt with first. However, the one with the fractured leg kept crying listlessly and complaining, '*Saab, bohut dorod ho raha hai* [Sir, it is hurting a lot].' His Hindi had an Oriya accent to it, so I asked him his name. He said that he was Havildar Sudhakar Panda. I assured him that we would take care of him and attend to his injury as soon as possible. After giving him a dose of morphine to alleviate the pain, I proceeded to the operation theatre to begin the surgery on the other serious injury.

The first casualty had a liver tear, and there was blood in the space between the coverings of the lungs. The surgery was done to repair his wounds, and then the patient was stabilised. It took us almost an hour and a half to finish everything, after which I asked for Havildar Panda to be wheeled in. He was brought in with an intravenous drip running into his left forearm. I decided to examine him again before surgery. He seemed quite comfortable, lying quietly on the bed. The effect of the morphine, I thought as I approached him. At close quarters, I realised that he appeared pale and there was no movement of his chest. He was not breathing.

We panicked. Resuscitation was started and injections were administered. It was all in vain. Havildar Panda had passed away. The cause of death was likely a massive bleed from the fracture of the femur. It could also have been a large fat embolism, but it was certainly not due to the morphine as a precise dose was given.

I slumped into a chair feeling miserable. I felt a tremendous sense of guilt for having failed the havildar. He had come to me for help, but I could not save him. Should I have had done his surgery first? But then, the liver injury had looked more serious. It ended in a disastrous situation.

I slowly walked back to my room and stared at the ceiling as I fretted about what else I could have done. Sleep was far away as I kept hearing the final words of Havildar Sudhakar Panda: '*Saab, bohut dorod ho raha hai.*'

23

The Major Returns

By the third week of July, my surgical workload was negligible. In fact, no casualties had arrived for two days. Though I was approaching the end of my tenure at Kargil, there was no word yet from Major Gambhir about his return. Only after he arrived back in Kargil would I be relieved of my duties here. As per the schedule, Major Gambhir was to be back in the next couple of days.

I compiled and summarised my daily reports and handed it to the commanding officer, who had sent a note of appreciation for my work at Kargil to the higher authorities. Although I was grateful for that, I did not know whether I deserved the appreciation. Anyone in my place would have done the same, or maybe even better. Perhaps the two fatalities under my charge could have been saved. I had just tried my best under the circumstances, with the Gita's advice — to perform one's duties no matter what — as my inspiration.

Major Gambhir returned on 22 July, marking the end of my surgical tenure at Kargil. The next day, our roles from the time I had arrived were reversed. It was I who was explaining all the cases and Major Gambhir the one patiently listening. After he had heard about my experiences and the kinds of surgeries I had performed, he said, 'Your cases have been reviewed by several hospitals after the patients were sent for recuperation to their various hometowns around the country. They all appreciated the surgical management done by you. Good job.'

Hearing that made me happy until the major suddenly put on a serious expression and said, 'The professor of surgery at our college in Pune was very concerned about something and wanted to get in touch with you as soon as possible.'

I felt anxious hearing this. Had something gone wrong with one of the cases? Had I committed a blunder? Could a patient have died due to my carelessness...

The Major Returns

Seeing my face, Major Gambhir added, 'Oh, it's nothing about your professional work. It's more personal.'

'What is it then?' I spluttered, unable to bear the suspense.

'Oh, there is a lady called Raveena who lives in Bombay,' said the major, trying to keep a straight face. 'It seems that she had visited Kargil and was so impressed by the surgeries done by a tall, bespectacled surgeon here that ever since she returned home she has been feeling lost, wanting to contact him again. She has been trying to get your number and address from the professor, so you had better contact him soon so that he can send it to her.'

That was my first good laugh in a while. 'You are too much,' I protested. 'For a while there, you scared the hell out of me!'

From the next day onward, I was relieved of my duties and Major Gambhir took over the ward. He was eager to get back to work after a long leave of absence. Given the low number of cases, he did not require any help, so I killed time by walking around chatting with the staff and having tea and soup with them. I realised that I was yet to eat the apricots the area was famous for and quickly plucked some from a tree. I also took the opportunity to visit the local market and even bought myself a Chinese-style jacket.

Though my involvement with the war effort was over, I knew the battles still raged on at the peaks. Soldiers were still dying even though people across India were already euphoric about our victory. In the cities, there were blood-donation camps, fundraisers, marches and other events being held in a show of support for the army.

I knew that it would all die down in a month or so and everyone would move on. The press would refocus their coverage to a new, different story. Most people would never hear about so many rank-and-file soldiers, the ones who continued to fight for their nation even if it meant losing their limbs or even their lives.

24

Flight to Srinagar

It was decided that I would leave Kargil on 24 July 1999. I had spent over two months here, a time that had coincided with the peak of Operation Vijay. To get back to my unit at Pattan, I had to travel by road to Leh and then take a flight to Chandigarh. From there, I'd have to fly again to Srinagar before travelling the last stretch by road. I was not looking forward to that tedious journey, so I went to the helipad at the back of the hospital to see if I could make alternative arrangements.

The helipad was a bustle of activity, with several young pilots busy at work. A little unsure, I asked if there was any chance of a helicopter going to Srinagar the next day. 'I'm looking to get there quickly,' I said. The pilots stopped their work and looked at me. 'If there is any person here who would get a priority airlift to Srinagar, it's you,' an officer said. 'And yes, there is an Mi-17 scheduled to fly to Srinagar tomorrow, weather permitting. Just fill up the form for the travel manifest.'

I was overjoyed, possibly more by the recognition from the officer than the prospect of the helicopter ride. When I had arrived here, I was practically a nobody. Now it seemed that my surgical exploits over the past two months had raised my status in the eyes of the people here. I thanked them and filled out the required paperwork.

I was no longer a surgeon at the Kargil field hospital and suddenly felt like a tourist. The town of Kargil seemed peaceful after a long time. I went back to the market and bought some trinkets and memorabilia for home along with a few packets of apricot kernels. Major Ramprasad arranged a small tea party for me in a corner of the ward, during which he gave a short speech of appreciation. I felt emotions in the air even though soldiers are not supposed to be the sentimental type and get attached to any place or person.

The next morning, I went to the ward for one last visit. The patients were having their breakfast and the nursing assistants were busy with their work. Life was going on as usual. The

Flight to Srinagar

ship would sail on but with a different captain at the helm. No one seemed to be bothered much about my leaving as I bid farewell to the staff. Then I went to say my goodbyes to the commanding officer. At the hospital entrance, I shook hands with Major Gambhir, who said that Major Ramprasad would accompany me to the helipad.

I cast one last look at the field hospital and began walking to the helipad. We heard the whirr of the rotor as an Mi-17 arrived carrying landmine casualties from the Batalik sector. They were being flown to Srinagar. Before I climbed into the aircraft, I turned to Major Ramprasad.

'So long, friend,' I said.

'Farewell, brother.'

We hugged each other. I felt heavy with emotion. Were his eyes moist too? I doubt it. The helicopter door was shut, the sound of the rotor increased and we slowly took off.

As we flew over the town of Kargil, I looked down at the market and the blue-domed mosque. Beside the national highway was the Suru river, flowing away towards the Line of Control. The helicopter made a turn and I could see the field hospital, the brigade headquarters and the Iqbal Bridge over the river. I remembered that that bridge was a hot target for the enemy and they had tried desperately to destroy it in an effort to cut the town off by severing connectivity to the highway. However, they had failed.

I then noticed the satellite telecommunication tower located behind the field hospital. Despite entry being prohibited, we used to sneak in there sometimes to make phone calls to our families as the long-distance phone at our hospital was often out of order. Depending on his mood, the supervisor would sometimes permit us to make calls. I reminisced about those phone calls, which had to be made after 10 p.m. as that was when the long-distance calling rates were the lowest.

The calls were always short because they were expensive and also because there were others waiting for their turn. I used to say things like 'I am fine, do not worry. We are all safe. You take care of yourselves.' My father would say, 'Keep steady and do your work. Keep at it. You're well protected by the Indian Army.' My mother would ask if I had eaten and if I had slept well. Finally, the phone would be handed to my wife, who would say in a soft voice, 'Take care, I miss you.'

Flight to Srinagar

We were soon flying at 15,000 feet. Kargil was behind us and ahead in the distance was the ice-clad sentinel of the Zanskar valley, the Nun peak. On both sides were barren mountains covered with snow. The helicopter negotiated the mountainous ridges and flew through small passes in the ranges. To my right, I noticed the small town of Dras. That area had witnessed the fiercest battles of the Kargil conflict. Many a civilian life had been lost due to Pakistani shelling.

Somewhere beyond those ridges ahead of us was the Line of Control. Among the peaks I could identify the famous Tiger Hill, the Tololing feature and Point 4875. From the helicopter they looked like small peaks that could be summited in a day or two. But the reality was entirely different. I tried to imagine a soldier climbing up those slopes with his load of ammunition, rations and equipment as he held on to the slippery, steep rock, directly in the line of enemy artillery, mortar and small-arms fire. On their charge towards the Line of Control, our soldiers had to survive on meagre rations and would sometimes go hungry for days on end. Yet they had ultimately managed to capture the peaks along the Line of Control.

The Kargil War Surgeon's Testimony

Though it seemed an impossible task to me, the indomitable Indian soldiers had achieved the impossible!

My thoughts went in a different direction, and I became pensive. That soft plea of help came to me again. 'It hurts a lot, sir...' the patient with the fractured leg had cried. I had failed to save him. Again, I wondered if I would ever be able to forgive myself and thought about the futility of war. The concept of war is based on an idea that others should be subjugated. Humans have a desire to dominate others and control and possess that which does not belong to them. This insatiable greed has led to history repeating itself time and again. And all of this stems from ego.

What could India have done in this scenario? Were we to sit back and allow the enemy to walk into our land, just because we are a nation of peace? Yes, we are the land of Gautam Buddha, Guru Nanak and Mahatma Gandhi. But we are also the land of Samudra Gupta, Rajendra Chola, Bhagat Singh and Subhas Chandra Bose. We have one of the best-trained armies in the world. So if an enemy starts a conflict with us, we will end it!

Flight to Srinagar

The helicopter flew above the national highway which was the chief target of the Pakistani artillery as it was the lifeline for the regions of Dras, Kargil and Leh. We flew through the famous Zoji La, which is the gateway from the Kashmir Valley to Ladakh. As soon as we had crossed the pass, the scenery all around us changed. The barren mountains were replaced by slopes covered in pine and other coniferous trees. Below us was a carpet of green grass, and small streams flowed turbulently in the gorges.

Over to the left, I could see the small village of Baltal, from which a path led to the Amarnath cave. In the distance were a couple of large waterbodies. I correctly identified them as Dal Lake and Nagin Lake. It meant we were close to Srinagar. The river Jhelum snaked through the city like a lazy earthworm. We flew over the Nagin Lake, and I spotted the Hazratbal mosque at the edge of the water. Then the boulevard around the perimeter of Dal Lake came into view, and I could see houseboats on the water. They looked like matchsticks in a puddle.

The helicopter landed in the Badami Bagh cantonment of Srinagar. It was as if I was back in civilisation. I headed straight to the Srinagar

The Kargil War Surgeon's Testimony

Base hospital and entered a bit apprehensively. I did not know how many of my cases had developed complications after their evacuation to Srinagar and wondered how the surgeons here would react to my presence.

There was a hubbub of activity at the casualty reception area as at least fifteen casualties had just arrived and were being attended to by the hospital staff. I noticed surgeons examining the patients as nurses noted down instructions. Medical officers were writing case sheets and paramedical staff were collecting blood samples. There was even a barber present, who was busy shaving the hair off the part of the body marked for surgery. I stood there watching but everybody was too engrossed in their work to pay me any attention.

Eventually, a medical officer noticed me and walked over. Upon reading my nameplate, he immediately called for some others. All of a sudden, I was the centre of attention. Someone brought me a chair while someone else offered me water. Then the doctors came to greet me. 'So you are the surgeon of Kargil,' said an orthopaedic surgeon. 'We have received many of your cases. They are all doing well. Excellent management of the cases!' A medical officer served me a cup of tea. After that, they went back to the patients, who were wheeled away to the operation theatre as I left the hospital.

My contribution to Operation Vijay had come to an end, but the days at Kargil kept coming back to me. I remembered the wailing and screaming of the severely wounded soldiers and seeing the partially burnt mortal remains of the ones who didn't make it. I lamented tragedies that had befallen Squadron Leader Ahuja and Captain Saurav Kalia and his men and shuddered as I recalled the details of how their bodies had been mutilated. The horrific accounts of the soldiers who had to survive for days by eating only snow and ice also came back to me. The memories made me sick. I had seen too much bloodshed and too many deaths. Yes, I had gained a lot of surgical experience, but I wondered whether it was worth it.

However, I was glad to hear that my patients had recovered and were doing well. During my two months at Kargil, I had managed about three hundred and fifty surgical casualties and had operated on over two hundred and fifty cases. There had only been two whom I could

The Kargil War Surgeon's Testimony

not save. Perhaps it could have gone better, but after my stint at Kargil, I felt more confident – no longer the apprehensive novice that I was before. I was still not too experienced but I knew that I would not be scared to perform surgery on complicated cases from now on.

25

The Suru's Eternal Flow

The Suru flowed beneath the Trishul peak of Kargil, skirted the Hathimatha feature and left the Kargil valley. It occasionally slowed as it flowed through flats and then picked up speed again as it lurched down a mountain. The river was tired of all that it had been forced to see – a mute witness to one of the avoidable tragedies of humankind. A tragedy created solely by man for the sake of the greed of a few – a ravenous greed to control the lives of other humans by dominating their land.

The Suru wondered why such preventable tragedies occurred time and again over the centuries. What prevented humans from learning from their mistakes? The Suru asked its mother, the glacier, but it had no answer. It then questioned its fellow rivers, the Stod, the Shingo, the Zanskar and the Dras. Their replies were mere mumbles from within their roaring waters. The Suru asked the lonely burnt fields it passed, the fish that lived in its own waters, the clear blue sky it flowed under and the friendly path that moved alongside and that lately had been ravaged by the heavy boots of soldiers. None of them had any answer.

But the river did not dare to ask the vainest of all species – humans. Probably they would not understand its language.

The Suru had seen the soldiers die on the mountain peaks – some shot, others blown to bits. Some had died from falls and others killed by the extreme climate of the winter months. The soldiers had no one to hear the stories of their hardships. Only the Suru gave them company from a distance.

The river saw the people of Kargil return to their broken homes and decided to forgive humans for destroying the peace and tranquil life of its valley. It tried to pacify them by washing the burnt fields and, with its gift of life-sustaining water, starting new growth in the lands all over again. It then washed the mountain slopes and cleaned the blood from them, washed away the tattered clothes of the soldiers and rinsed the surroundings with its fresh waters.

The Suru's Eternal Flow

However, the Suru still remained confused about why the tragedies had to happen and whether they would ever end.

That was when the river heard a strange sound. There were human voices speaking various unknown languages. Hundreds of voices, whispering, mumbling, all of them trying to tell the river something. The Suru found that it could understand what they were saying. The humans had come from all corners of the country. One was from a village near Thiruvananthapuram in Kerala and another from the hilly area of Bomdila in Arunachal Pradesh. Some had their origins in the ravines of Chambal region in Madhya Pradesh while others hailed from the dense forests of Khunti in Jharkhand. They could confide only in the river, as no one else could ever hear their stories.

The voices spoke about how they had braved the mountainous terrain and protected their land from the intruders. The Suru heard every word about their feelings and about the realities of war. It tried to understand the emotional bonds they had with their families. Thanking them all for their efforts, it prayed for the peace of their souls and courage for their families.

The Kargil War Surgeon's Testimony

The voices kept fading away, but the Suru could hear questions being asked by some of them.

Why did our neighbours have to tread into our territory, the territory that never belonged to them? Why are they so obsessed about taking this land instead of developing their own land? Why did they cause so much destruction? Was it all worth it?

The river heard them ask what they were supposed to do when it happened. Were they to stand a mute witness and let them pillage and plunder the land the humans shared with the Suru? *Did we not do right in defending your vale?* asked the voices. *Yet, what did we, or they, learn from all this? Nothing, isn't it? Why have they kept repeating the same mistake time and again ever since their nation was created?*

The Suru could not answer them. It flowed on silently as the voices faded away.

A little later, the Suru heard another faint voice from far away. It belonged to a young man from Palampur in Himachal Pradesh. More a boy than a man, really – he had been only twenty-two and had joined the Indian Army only six months before the Kargil conflict. He seemed to be struggling to speak as he said in a hushed voice: *Have you forgotten us too, Suru, as*

The Suru's Eternal Flow

all the others have? Do you also feel that we were careless during our patrol or were foolhardy, as some say about us? Without any prior experience in your land, the six of us were sent on a patrol. How much did we know about the mountainous terrain of the region?

The voice told the Suru that their patrol had not disobeyed any order and had tried their best but had been caught unawares and outnumbered by the enemy. *Did you hear our cries when they burnt our skins with cigarettes? I could do nothing for Arjun Ram and Tularam when they pierced their eardrums with a hot iron rod. Then they plucked out our nails and broke our hands.*

Naresh Singh and Bhanwar Lal had cried, 'Why are they doing this to us? What do they hope to achieve?' Then Tikaram's eyes were gouged out, and his skull cracked by a rod. I had to see it all. But even when they had stomped on my chest with their heavy boots and yelled, 'Shout Hindustan Murdabad!' I had not uttered a word. And so they cut off my penis and shot me several times. They transformed my body into a tattered sieve. I was never afraid of dying in a war ... but do you think that I deserved to die this way?

The Kargil War Surgeon's Testimony

The Suru heard the voice say that only a few in his country would remember them. Perhaps only their families. The rest would forget. *Suru, you should forget us too. Why should you remember this tale, when my countrymen have forgotten me?* Then the voice faded away, never to be heard again.

The Suru river heard it all in silence as it moved on in its eternal flow.

Acknowledgements

I would be failing in my duties if I did not thank the people without whom this book would not have seen the light of day.

To all those fallen soldiers whose stories changed my outlook towards life and to all those wounded soldiers I had the privilege to treat, I offer my heartfelt thanks. I am grateful that I could serve them, and this book is an outcome of my interactions with them. I offer my thanks to the Army Medical Corps (AMC) for having confidence in me and allowing me to serve in a difficult field area in the midst of an armed conflict. I also thank the Government of India for allowing me to serve as an officer of the Indian Army.

My parents were my first teachers, and they were instrumental in shaping me and providing me with a good education. They taught me humanism, tolerance and ethics and the lesson that life does not revolve around a career. I am proud to be their son.

Acknowledgements

I am indebted to my medical school, the Armed Forces Medical College, Pune, for giving me a rock-solid foundation in the practice of medicine and the art of surgery and to all the teachers of my alma mater.

I would like to thank Major General Balachandran Nambiar, AVSM, SM, VSM of the AMC; and Major General Vikram Taneja, VSM of the AOC, who went beyond the call of duty to help get this book published. I am grateful to them. I am also indebted to Jaya Bhattacharji Rose of Ace Literary Consulting and Raja Bose, both of whom suggested various improvements to the book and ensured that it gets published. Sincere thanks to Bloomsbury India for publishing my book.

I offer heartfelt thanks to my wife, Sruti, who despite her busy schedule as a teacher, social worker and Bharatanatyam dancer took time out to read and reread the manuscript and make significant improvements.

I remain forever grateful to all my readers for your encouragement.

About the Author

Arup Ratan Basu received an MBBS degree from the Armed Forces Medical College, Pune, after his schooling from Loyola School and DBMS English School, Jamshedpur. He joined the Army Medical Corps in 1989 and completed a master's in surgery and post-doctoral fellowship in gastro-intestinal surgery. During the Kargil conflict of 1999, he was deputed as a general surgeon to the field hospital in Kargil, and he received the Yuddh Seva Medal for his services there. In 2001 he was deputed to Kabul, Afghanistan, immediately after the collapse of the first Taliban regime. He served there for ten months and was awarded a certificate of appreciation by the government of Afghanistan. Later, he served in various command hospitals of the Army Medical Corps and settled down in his hometown, Jamshedpur, in 2013.

Basu has written three books in Bengali. This is his first book in English.